ALSO BY *Graham Blackburn*

Illustrated Housebuilding

The Illustrated Encyclopedia of Woodworking Handtools, Instruments & Devices

Illustrated Basic Carpentry

The Postage Stamp Gazetteer

Illustrated Furniture Making

Illustrated Interior Carpentry

The Illustrated Encyclopedia of Ships, Boats, Vessels, and other water-borne Craft

The Illustrated Dictionary of Nautical Terms

The Parts of a House

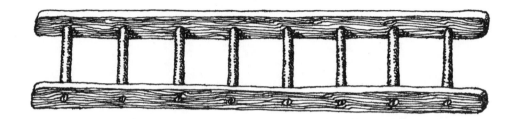

Now, if your buildings have been neglected, and are all dilapidated; if you have chosen rather to sit by the fire and count your fingers, than to take the hammer and drive a few nails; or if you have been in the habit of hanging round Peter Fogo's grog-shop, to the disregard of your home affairs, then you are indeed a sufferer.

Whew! how the wind blows! Crack, slap, rip up and tear all! Your old hovel is about taking its departure amidst the posting winds.

FROM THE FARMER'S ALMANAC PUBLISHED IN NEW ENGLAND
1835

An Illustrated Calendar of HOME REPAIR

by Graham Blackburn

RICHARD MAREK PUBLISHERS
New York

Richard Marek Publishers, Inc.
200 Madison Avenue
New York, New York
1 0 0 1 6

LIBRARY OF CONGRESS CATALOGING IN PUBLICATION DATA
Blackburn, Graham, 1940-
    An illustrated calendar of home repair.

Bibliography : p.
Includes index.
1. Dwellings — Maintenance and repair.   I. Title.
TH 4817. B55   643'.6   80-16026
ISBN 0-399-90094-2

Designed by Graham Blackburn

Printed in the United States of America

for
Basia
& her new house

C O N T E N T S

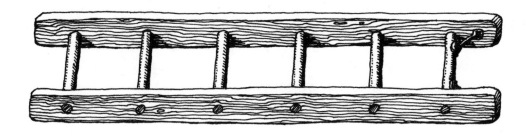

CONTENTS

CONTENTS

INTRODUCTION

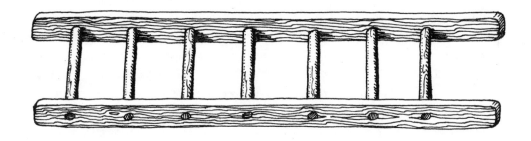

This book has been designed as a kind of service manual for your home. There are many jobs to be done at various times throughout the year and it is easy to forget something until it is too late; and even if all the jobs could be done at the same time, you would have to completely stop the rest of your life for the duration. Few of us have the time or the inclination for this.

The **Calendar** tells you when certain jobs are best done, month by month, and to make life easy, splits up the remaining jobs (which might well be taken care of at any time) and distributes them as evenly and as logically as possible with the first group.

At the beginning of each month there is a checklist which enables you to see at a glance what ought to be done and what has been done. There is space for you to keep a record for at least ten years, so that if you miss something one year you will be able to see exactly when it was done last. There is also more space in each month's checklist for other jobs you might want to add on a monthly or an annual basis.

INTRODUCTION

Although there is a lot of detailed information on how to do various things, the main purpose of the **Calendar** is not so much a technical treatise on practical building and carpentry as it is a guide for the maintenance of a house. It does not even imply that you are necessarily the one to perform the maintenance or actually effect any repairs; merely that a knowledge of what is necessary is gained, together with an understanding of what constitutes a good and satisfactory job.

In the event that you cannot resist the urge to tackle something (or everything) yourself, I have included a bibliography of more detailed texts on the several aspects of building and home maintenance.

Furthermore, everything is indexed in alphabetical order at the back of the book, so if you suddenley have doubts about the foundation, for example, you do not have to read through the whole year to find out about it.

So aside from unexpected catastrophes such as earthquakes and atom bombs, a periodic brief glance at the **Calendar** will ensure that over the course of any twelve-month cycle everything will have received attention at least once, and you can enjoy your home instead of worrying about it.

Graham Blackburn
THE CROWN & ANCHOR
W O O D S T O C K
New York   1980

An Illustrated
Calendar of
HOME REPAIR
from
JANUARY
to
DECEMBER

THINGS TO CHECK	YEAR										
EAVES *for ice dams and blocked gutters*											
FURNITURE *for insufficient humidity*											
TOOLS, HOUSEHOLD & GARDEN *for repair or replacement*											

ANNUAL CHECKLIST OF HOME REPAIR FOR JANUARY

J A N U A R Y

ICICLES &
ICE DAMS·
HUMIDITY
IN THE
HOUSE·
ON TOOLS
IN GENERAL·

JANUARY

January should be an easy month around the house. The holidays are over and your newly made resolutions should hold good for at least the first month. There is no grass to mow and it's too cold to paint the house, so look forward to a lot of cosy time spent around the fire.

If the weather is freezing, but there has not been too much snow, there should be plenty of ice about, which makes for great ice-skating, but which can lead to problems with the roof. So the next time you leave the house on a sunny day for an afternoon on the pond take a look at the bottom edge of the roof - the eaves.

ICE DAMS

Sunny weather melts any snow on the roof but if the temperature is still down around freezing the melted snow quickly forms icicles at the edge of the roof. This looks pretty but can lead to problems with the roof (not to mention speared heads for the unwary).

As the thaw-and-freeze cycle continues, the icicles grow larger and at their upper end form a wall of ice along the edge of the roof. This wall of ice is known as an ice dam, for it dams up water that would otherwise run off the roof and causes it to seep back under the shingles and down into your house.

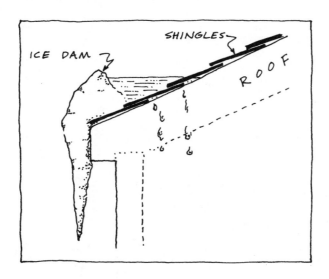

The biggest factor in the buildup of ice dams is an uninsulated or insufficiently insulated roof. Heat from the interior of the house passes through the roof and melts any snow, but the edge of the roof, which usually overhangs the outside wall a little, is not thus warmed and so remains frozen.

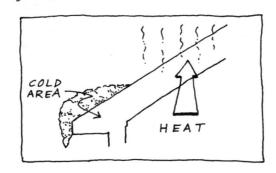

T he first thing to do is to make sure your roof is indeed insulated (see **OCTOBER** for details of roof insulation). A well-insulated roof should keep most of its snow cover (since no heat is escaping through the roof to melt it), and this in turn acts as an additional blanket of insulation. Of course, in areas of heavy snowfall roofs are generally built with a steeper pitch (slope) than elsewhere, in order that excessive amounts of snow may slide off rather than collapsing the roof, although some should still remain. If, a short while after a snowfall, you can see patches of your roof, this is a good indication you are losing heat through the roof.

A nother thing to check is that protruding gutters do not impede the run off. While gutters should be positioned to catch run off, they ought to lie behind the slope of the roof, as shown opposite, otherwise they will catch snow that slides down the roof, which can then build up and possibly cause an ice dam. For the same reason gutters should be kept cleaned out and free from obstructions such as dead leaves.

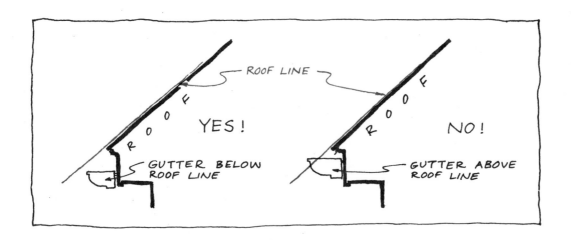

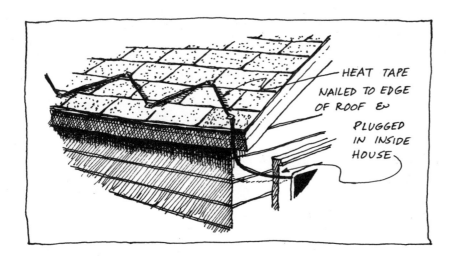

owever, even if your roof is adequately pitched, your insulation sufficient, and your gutters properly positioned, ice dams may still occur. Then the cure is to install a heat tape along the bottom edge of the roof to melt any incipient ice buildup.

O f interest is the way in which the problem of ice dams was often solved in pre-electric days. The eaves were finished with a broad band of tin so that even if an ice dam did form there would be no shingles for trapped water to work back under. Hand in hand with this solution often went the practice of installing projections on the roof to hinder the snow from sliding off, since it formed useful insulation.

VICTORIAN HOUSE WITH TIN EAVES

HUMIDITY

By now the heating system probably will have been going full blast for a while, and the moisture content of the house will have reached its winter level. It is important to take note of this because too much or too little moisture in the air can have deleterious effects on you, your house, and the things in it – especially wooden furniture.

Very simply, moisture in the air cuts heating costs and increases comfort by making the temperature in the house more uniform. Insufficient moisture or humidity can dry out you and your furniture (causing the latter to shrink and crack), and excessive humidity can lead to condensation problems such as rotted woodwork and stained ceilings and walls.

People with expensive wooden furniture and high-quality pianos and other wooden instruments must often take extensive precautions to control the humidity in order to avoid damage. Even your sturdy family piano will exhibit dramatic changes in pitch when subjected to changes in humidity, and unless you keep a sharp eye on the hygrometer and heed its warnings, the piano tuner will be a too frequent visitor.

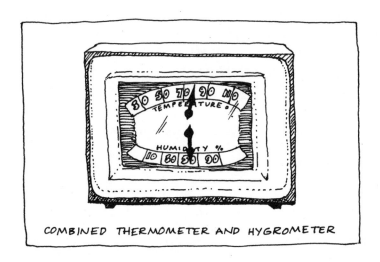

COMBINED THERMOMETER AND HYGROMETER

The hygrometer is an inexpensive instrument for measuring the humidity in your house. Hygrometers are very often included with thermometers, to which they may look very similar, and are often designed to hang on a wall or sit on a shelf.

The needle of the hygrometer points not to degrees of temperature but to the percent moisture content of the surrounding air.

If you see cracks appearing in unfinished (or even finished) wooden surfaces, if the gap between cupboard or cabinet doors and their frames seems to be widening, and if you wake up parched and thirsty every morning, then the hygrometer's needle will be pointing to a very low number. On the other hand, if every time the temperature drops outside, your windows drip with water on the inside, and your supply of postage stamps is all stuck together, and every door in the house becomes hard to open, then you will observe a very high reading on the hygrometer.

A lot depends on the kind of heating system you use. A wood stove will dry out the moisture in the air very quickly — for which reason many people often keep large kettles of water simmering on top of the stove — the steam thus produced helps to replace the evaporated moisture in the air.

Similarly, hot-air heating-systems can be very drying, although if the cold-air-return part of the system is located in a damp basement, this dampness will be pumped into the house as moisture in the hot air. This is not often the case however, since the cold-air return is usually located within the house, and in this situation the only cure is to install a humidifier in the hot-air system, whereby the hot air can be kept at the desired level of humidity.

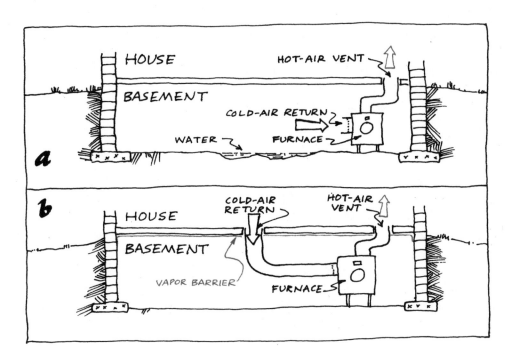

a   A hot-air system drawing in damp air from the basement and pumping moist hot air into the house.

b   A hot-air system which gets its cold air from within the house, heats it, and pumps it back into the house. The basement, even if it was damp, is separated from the house (and the cold-air return) by a vapor barrier.

Electric heat is less drying than hot air, but the most comfortable of all is a hot-water system, using either radiators or baseboard units. In any event, you will probably not be able to change your heating system so if it is too drying the only thing to do is to install a humidifier to put back the lost moisture.

If your problem is too much humidity you can always install a dehumidifier – usually in the basement, since this is likely to be the source of the excess moisture. If your heating system does not draw air from the basement (because it is a closed system like electric or hot-water), then installing a vapor barrier between the basement and the house will help (as shown at **b** on the previous page).

Every house should be built with vapor barriers surrounding the living space, in order to prevent condensation forming in the walls and the roof. Even a house with a comfortable and correct humidity level will still have enough moisture in the air to cause condensation when it comes into contact with cold exterior walls. Theoretically, the house should be insulated well enough so that the warm air inside does not reach the inside surfaces of the immediate exterior of the house, but this is rarely possible.

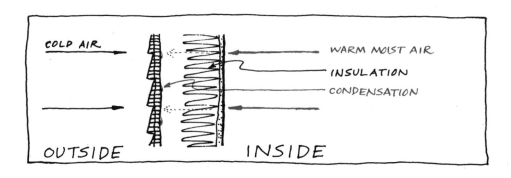

COLD AIR   WARM MOIST AIR
            INSULATION
            CONDENSATION

OUTSIDE   INSIDE

T he only way to prevent such condensation forming on the inside surfaces of the house's exterior covering is some form of vapor barrier between the insulation and the interior wall or ceiling.

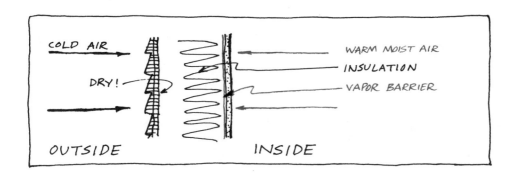

COLD AIR →

DRY! →

WARM MOIST AIR

INSULATION

VAPOR BARRIER

OUTSIDE   INSIDE

S ome fiberglass insulation is sold with paper or foil backing, which is supposed to reflect heat back into the house and act as a vapor barrier. It may do the former, but it cannot do the latter unless it is continuous over the whole surface of the wall or ceiling in question. Even the slightest gap or unsealed joint between rolls (of insulation), not to mention tears in the foil or backing, will allow moist air through. The only effective barrier is a skin of plastic sheeting around the entire room just underneath the finished wall, overlapping well and taped at the joints between sheets.

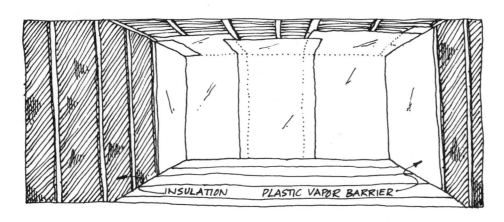

INSULATION   PLASTIC VAPOR BARRIER

Windows, of course, present a gap in the vapor barrier and can be the first places where condensation is observed. The warm moist inside air hits the glass, made cold from the outside, and immediately the moisture condenses into water droplets and runs down the inside of the window. As it gets even colder outside, this condensed moisture can freeze, and you can wake up to find a layer of ice covering the inside of your windows!

As if this isn't unpleasant enough on a cold and chilly morning, when you turn the thermostat up or get the fire going, the temperature rises inside and all this ice melts and can cause quite a mess, not to mention the eventual deterioration of your window's woodwork.

The cure here is storm windows or double glazing. (Or the temporary measure of a sheet of plastic tacked up over the entire window, on the inside or the outside, it doesn't matter which, except that tacked up inside, the plastic is less likely to blow away in a winter storm!) The principle behind two layers of glass (or a layer of glass and a layer of plastic) is that the inner sandwich of air prevents the cold from the outside reaching the inside glass, and the moist interior air from reaching the cold outer glass. This of course not only solves your condensation problem, but is at the same time excellent and basic insulation also saving heat. For more information on storm windows, see SEPTEMBER.

Installing a vapor barrier after a house is finished is a big job since it involves removing all the interior surfaces again. So until this is undertaken the only solution to excessive humidity is a dehumidifier. Remember, controlling the humidity and keeping all the moisture in the air inside the house is the best thing you can do for your exterior walls and roof. Over the years condensation will cause rot and decay and peeling paint on the outside of the house.

TOOLS

The purpose of this book is not so much a treatise on practical building or carpentry as it is a guide for the maintenance of a house. It does not even imply that the reader is necessarily the one to actually perform any maintenance or effect any repairs, merely that a knowledge of what is necessary is gained together with an understanding of what constitutes a good and satisfactory job.

YOUR ONLY TOOL?

Nevertheless, rare is the person who will not at one time or another pick up a hammer or a screwdriver, and whether <u>you</u> do the work or not, every house should possess a few basic tools. Therefore, a few words on the kind of tools that ought to be found around the house is in order.

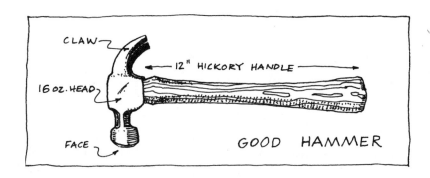

CLAW

12" HICKORY HANDLE

16 OZ. HEAD

FACE

GOOD HAMMER

The most important thing to be said about tools is that cheap, poor quality tools are worse than useless. A hammer that breaks or bends the first time you use it, or a screwdriver that twists like a pretzel, is not worth even the very small amount it may have cost. Not only will such a tool not do its job, thereby frustrating or discouraging you, but it may even be downright dangerous. So even if all you have in the house is one hammer, have a good one at least. If you know nothing about tools, it is simply a matter of asking for "the best" at the ironmonger's or hardware store.

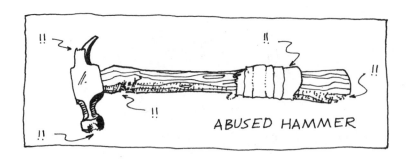

!!

!!

!!

!!

!!

ABUSED HAMMER

The next most important thing to be said about tools is that although they are designed to do a lot of work, and some of it very hard work, there are very few tools which will remain at all useful if they are abused or even simply not given a little attention once in a while.

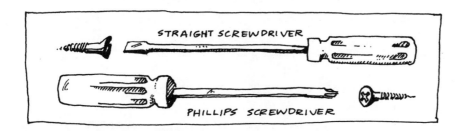

side from a hammer and a couple of screwdrivers (a straight screwdriver and a phillips screwdriver for those screws which are made not with slots in their heads but with crosses), try and equip the house with a pair of pliers, an adjustable wrench, and an electric drill and a set of drill bits.

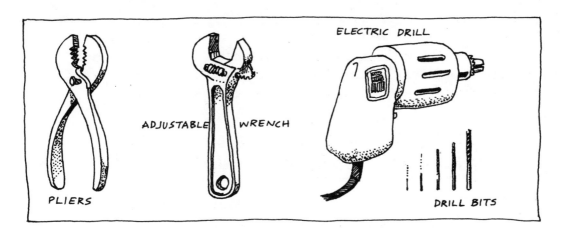

These few tools will enable you to effect practically all emergency repairs, at least temporarily, and will also be found useful dozens of times for small jobs such as hanging pictures, screwing the radio antenna on, and tightening a loose nut on the vacuum cleaner. If you include a saw, any kind from a hacksaw to a handsaw, and a metal tape measure, you will have a complete basic toolkit (and will be able to saw down your own Christmas tree to the correct height!).

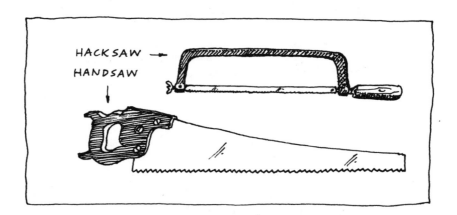

This list of tools really is the absolute minimum because even if _you_ don't want to do anything around the house, these tools will enable any willing friend to render assistance and save some hefty bills from visiting professionals such as plumbers, electricians, and carpenters.

8 BASIC HOUSEHOLD TOOLS :	
HAMMER	ADJUSTABLE WRENCH
STRAIGHT SCREWDRIVER	ELECTRIC DRILL & BITS
PHILLIPS SCREWDRIVER	SAW
PLIERS	TAPE MEASURE

JANUARY

Anyone interested enough to go beyond this list probably enjoys tools for their own sake and also has an interest in carpentry and fixing things, and will undoubtedly discover, or have discovered already, the almost infinite number of tools which have been designed for every conceivable application.

For the rest all that remains to be said is that it is a good idea to check up on your tools once in a while (and January is an ideal month since there is not much else to do, and it can be a nice, warm, indoor job). Provide them with a home of their own which is readily accessible, such as a cupboard under the stairs, and try and hang as many of them up as possible rather than throwing them all together in a box.

A well-organized toolbox may well be the hallmark of a fine craftsman, but a small collection of household tools tends to get lost and damaged in a box stuffed under the sink or at the back of the linen closet. The one tool you want is invariably buried under all the other tools, and you not only scratch your hand trying to extricate it, but often bend, blunt, or otherwise damage the tool itself.

Take the time now to make sure all tools are present and hung up where they should be. Squirt a drop of oil on joints and moving parts. Make sure there is no rust anywhere — if there is, rub it off with fine wire wool. Make sure the hammer head is not loose — if it is, and it has a wooden handle, go to the hardware store and buy an extra wedge to drive in the end; and file the end of the straight screwdriver straight again if it should happen to have become rounded over.

THINGS TO CHECK	YEAR										
OUTSIDE for snow damage											
GLUED SURFACES for adhesion											
LOCKS, HINGES, & RELATED HARDWARE for good operation & security											
FLOORS for shrinking, swelling, squeaking, & sagging											

ANNUAL CHECKLIST OF HOME REPAIR FOR **FEBRUARY**

F E B R U A R Y

SNOW & ICE &
BUSHES & BIRDS ·
ON GLUE & STICK-
ING THINGS TOGETHER ·
ON LOCKS & HINGES
& UNSTICKING THINGS ·
ON FLOORS ·

FEBRUARY

Winter deepens and the memories of holidays fade, but now is the time to look ahead. Although the days may be bitterly cold and the nights seem interminably long, daylight is actually increasing, and by larger amounts every day. Many seed catalogs offer discounts if you order before the end of February. Yes, Spring is that close, and bringing a branch of forsythia or apple tree indoors and setting it in water will demonstrate this fact with glorious bloom.

OUTSIDE

There is, in fact, from this point on, an increasing amount to be done outside the house, even for those with the smallest of grounds and gardens. After snowstorms, shake the snow with care from evergreen bushes and hedges to prevent the branches from breaking. Be especially careful if it is very cold, for frozen branches are brittle and can be easily broken. At the same time stamp the snow down firmly around fruit trees and other special trees to prevent little rodents tunneling in to feed off the bark.

If you enjoy the birds then feed them; they will especially appreciate feeding immediately after a storm. And if you stand your old Christmas tree upside down in the snow you can provide some welcome extra shelter. However, if you do start feeding the birds don't stop in mid-Winter for they will have become dependent on you.

Ashes from the fireplace or stove not used for making icy paths and steps safe should be used for garden compost, especially hardwood ashes, which are a very rich soil builder. It is true that commercially sold salt works better at melting treacherous ice, and that ashes can become messy, but bear in mind that the salt has a bad effect on concrete and cement, slowly helping to disintegrate it, so do not be overly generous with the salt.

FEBRUARY

GLUING In addition to the warnings about excessive dryness of the air in the house caused by heating systems, given in JANUARY, there are a few other possible side effects to watch for that serve to introduce the topic of glue and gluing.

C heck glued surfaces to see if they are still stuck. Inspect kitchen tiles, wall and floor, especially the non-ceramic kinds such as asphalt, rubber, or vinyl-asbestos tiles. Old woodwork, where glued, was glued with animal glues which can become brittle with age and which do not always stand up well to heat.

1 f, on inspecting the woodwork, especially old furniture, you find that parts are loose, you should reglue them. Look for loose corner blocks in the inside corners of tables, chairs, and cabinets, loose rungs in chairs, and unstuck pieces of veneer on table tops and furniture such as wardrobes.

BLOCKS

CORNER BLOCKS WHICH
CAN BECOME UNGLUED

FEBRUARY

T here are two important things to remember when gluing. Firstly, make sure both surfaces are clean — this includes scraping off any traces of the old glue if you are regluing — and secondly, use the right glue for the job.

T he six kinds of glue that you are likely to need and may encounter in the hardware store are as follows:

1. Animal-hide or fish glues. Now usually sold ready mixed, this is the old-time glue once exclusively used by cabinetmakers who had to boil it in a double gluepot to prepare it for use. Satisfactory so long as no dampness or excessive heat is present, but capable of staining light wood, animal glue is now little used because the following types are far more convenient in a variety of ways.

2. White polyvinyl acetate glues. These are the familiar milky-white glues often sold in squeezable plastic containers. They are good for all interior woodworking jobs where waterproofing is not called for. They are also good for a variety of other substances such as paper, leather, cork, and fabric.

3. Plastic resin glues. These come as powder which must be mixed with water before use and which then form a strong and waterproof joint for all kinds of woodwork. Joints must, however, be firmly clamped while the glue sets.

4. Waterproof resorcinol glues. A two-part glue, consisting of a powdered catalyst and a liquid resin which are mixed together just before use; this is the ideal glue for very strong exterior joints.

5. Epoxy adhesives. The strongest of all, these are also two-part glues consisting of resin and catalyst (hardener). Epoxy when set is hard, waterproof, and permanent. It is also generally available in small quantities or large, thus making it ideal for small jobs such as gluing china or glass, and bigger jobs that involve patching — since the epoxy can be used as a filler and filed down afterwards.

6. Contact cement. Two types of contact cement exist: a solvent-thinned cement which is very flammable, and a water-thinned variety which is not flammable and which does not give off toxic odors. Contact cement is especially useful for gluing awkwardly-shaped or positioned objects which are not readily susceptible to clamping, since it grips on contact — although both surfaces must be allowed to dry the requisite amount before being brought together.

7 In addition to excessive dryness and heat causing glued surfaces to become unstuck, the opposite condition — of dampness — can also have the same effect, so run a "sticking check" after an unusually damp period, such as lengthy spring rains or a spell of humid weather.

LOCKS AND HINGES

This is a good time of year to attend to the opposite problem from the previous one of gluing back together unstuck things — the unsticking of things that ought to move freely, i.e., locks and hinges.

While occurring more frequently with automobiles than houses, locks can become inoperable as a result of wetness followed by extreme cold. It is an extremely tiresome experience to have to stand in the cold, trying to warm up a key over a match (usually with a wind blowing) in order to melt a frozen door lock (by inserting the hot key into it). So practise a little periodic prevention by applying liquid graphite to the key and working it in and out of all your exterior locks. Graphite has the twofold effect of helping to prevent freezing and providing a general lubrication which will make the lock last longer and easier to operate.

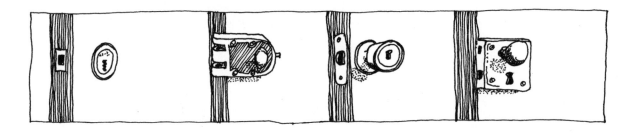

A lock which is still hard to operate after an oiling may need cleaning. There may be an accumulation of too much old grease and dirt clogging up the works. Carefully remove and disassemble the lock and clean it thoroughly (with an old toothbrush and some solvent, like gasoline). On reassembly, lightly oil it and try again. If it is still hard to work it is either wrongly assembled (you may have screwed something in too tightly) or simply too old and worn and should be replaced.

Pay particular attention to tubular locks (the Kwikset type), the retaining screws of which sometimes work loose — but at the same time make sure that the bolt still springs in and out and is not bound because you have tightened the screws too much.

On your tour of inspection of locks, carry a screwdriver with you and make sure all the screws holding all the hinges for doors, windows, and cabinets are tight. It is surprising how much some of these screws can work loose, leading to hard-to-close doors, etc.

otice that some hinges have removable pins holding the two leaves together, and these sometimes work up and threaten to fall out. Tap them back in!

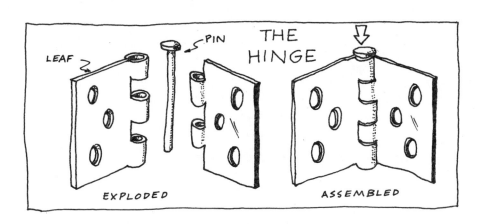

LEAF — PIN — THE HINGE

EXPLODED · ASSEMBLED

 se the screwdriver to check that all the catches, locks, handles, and fasteners are still tightly screwed in place. One more related job which is convenient to do at this time is to check all the wooden handles in drawers and doors, etc. Some are glued in place (and may need to be reglued - see the previous section), and some are held by screws which may need a tightening.

SCREW · SCREW · SCREW · GLUE · SCREW

FLOORS

At this time of year some floor problems may be more evident than at other times, so this is a good month to discuss common floor problems in general. Apart from a trauma-type injury to a floor, such as fire burning a hole in it or a piano falling through it (in which case major reconstruction is called for), the typical problems which can afflict a floor are as follows:

SHRINKING
SWELLING
SQUEAKING
SAGGING

Gaps between floorboards, caused by the wood shrinking, are most likely to show up at this time of year because this is when the house is likely to be at its driest. There is little that can be done for narrow-board hardwood floors, but the problem is most likely to occur with wider-board softwood floors such as pine anyway, for which there is some help.

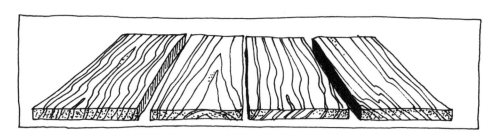

Firstly, unless the floor is new, in which case shrinkage probably reflects the wood's natural seasoning (which ideally should have been accomplished before it was laid), a seasonal shrinking (and subsequent swelling) indicates a lack of sufficient humidity control (see JANUARY). This situation can be helped at the floor itself by sealing the wood with some kind of finish, thereby making it more impervious to moisture.

Secondly, if the floor is relatively old, and there are gaps of up to half an inch or more between boards, it is possible to fill these with wedge-shaped fillets of any available wood (the same color might be preferable). Make sure that the thick edge of the wedge is larger than the gap; pound the fillet in, using a block of scrap wood as shown; and then plane or sand the whole thing level.

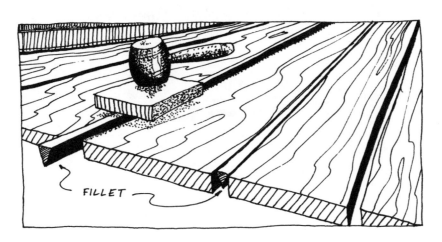

FILLET

Swelling and buckling of the floorboards is caused by too much moisture in the floor, such as rain damage or a plumbing leak, and is a little more serious than shrinking.

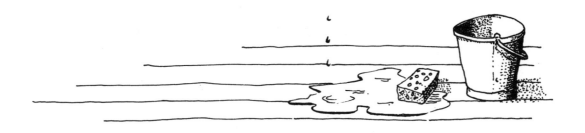

You can try drying the wood, using a heat lamp, and then attempt to flatten the floorboards again either by nailing through into the joist below or by screwing up through the subfloor from underneath.

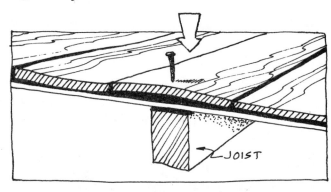

For more serious swelling that can no longer be reduced enough by drying you will just have to remove a board and replace it with a narrower one. This more frequently occurs with narrow, tongue-and-groove flooring.

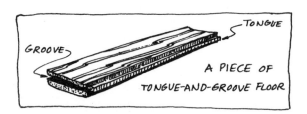

When a section of tongue-and-groove flooring has buckled, especially the narrower, hardwood types, it should not prove too difficult to pull or pry one board loose. But try to avoid damaging the edges of the adjacent boards. If there is any danger of this, try splitting the board to be removed along its center with a chisel, and pry it free from this point. After flattening the remaining boards as described earlier, replace the missing board with a piece fractionally larger than the vacant space — in order to produce a snug fit.

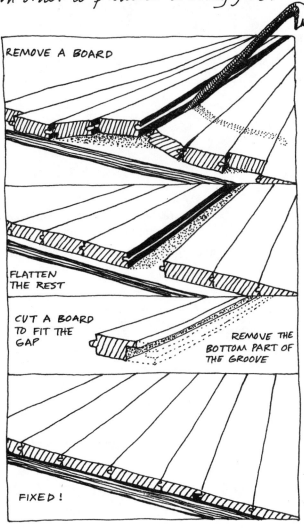

REMOVE A BOARD

FLATTEN
THE REST

CUT A BOARD
TO FIT THE
GAP

REMOVE THE
BOTTOM PART OF
THE GROOVE

FIXED!

Squeaking floors are usually the result of loose floorboards. If the floor is surface-nailed, make sure all the nails are hammered home at least flush with the surface of the floor, and preferably set a little below the surface (using a nailset to avoid making hammer marks —called moons— on the floor).

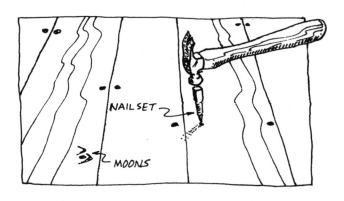

Even if the floor is not surface-nailed, you could try surface-nailing the squeaking part anyway, just taking care to set the nail as shown above, and filling the hole with plastic wood. Two nails driven in at opposing angles work best.

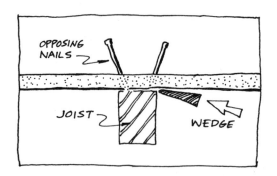

Another cure is to wedge the floor from underneath — if you can get to it — between the offending part and the joist on which it is supposed to rest.

S agging is most easily curable if it occurs on the first floor (or ground floor as it is referred to in Britain), for then it may be supported from below and jacked up level again. If there is sufficient space (as in a basement, but not in a crawlspace) you can use a metal column of the type which may be adjusted up or down by screwing. The important thing here is to do it slowly — no more than half an inch per week! This allows everything to readjust gradually without exerting any sudden and potentially damaging strain on the rest of the structure.

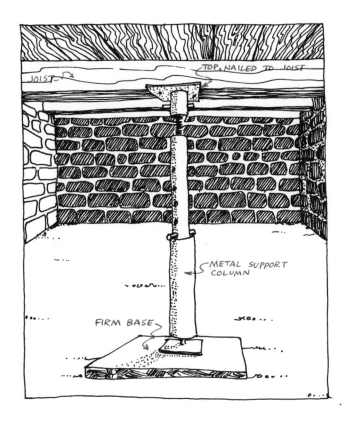

JOIST

TOP, NAILED TO JOIST

METAL SUPPORT COLUMN

FIRM BASE

1 f a higher floor is sagging and it is not possible to erect a post under it, there is little you can do, except maybe remove as much weight as possible, short of installing new or additional joists.

THINGS TO CHECK	YEAR											
GUTTERS *for breaks, obstructions, correct slope, holes, & leaks*												
HOUSE SITE *for standing water, heaved ground, & cracked paths*												
CULVERTS & DITCHES *for free flow*												
FUEL TANKS *for shifting position*												

ANNUAL CHECKLIST OF HOME REPAIRS FOR **MARCH**

M A R C H

AFTER THE SNOW:
GUTTERS·
SITE DRAINAGE·
CULVERTS &
DITCHES·
GAS, OIL, &
WATER TANKS·

Even if March in many areas is not quite Spring (despite the seemingly arbitrary pronouncements of the almanac), it may often be fairly treated as the end of Winter, and certain Spring jobs can be contemplated, although they may have to be put aside from time to time as Winter attempts a few last comebacks.

As the snow disappears, the outside will begin to claim more of your time. Gardeners can remove the mulch from snowdrops and crocuses, and prune their fruit trees. Trellises should be repaired and painted, if necessary, before they begin to be covered by vines and climbing plants, and you can begin to clear up in general — broken branches, things that got buried under the snow, etc.

GUTTERS

One part of the house which may have suffered during the Winter, especially if there has been a lot of snow and ice, and which may shortly be needed more than at any other time of the year, is the roof-runoff system — the gutters and downspouts. If gutters have been damaged by heavy snow loads, and downspouts become disconnected or clogged up, heavy Spring rains can wreak havoc with foundation plantings and considerably impair the drainage situation around the house.

he whole idea behind gutters is to collect the rain that falls on the roof and conduct it away safely – and even usefully, as into a rainbarrel or storage tank for use during dry times or because it may be softer than your tapwater.* If allowed to run off all around the roof, not only will you get rain down your neck as you come and go, but eventually a substantial trench may be eroded around the house to the detriment of both plants and the foundation.

he damage to plants is obvious – they will simply be washed away. The damage to the foundation is a little more subtle.

FLOWERS

TRENCH

BEFORE   AFTER

* Beware of using rainwater collected from a roof that has been newly reshingled with asphalt shingles – it may be full of the surfacing granules, some of which wash off at first. Similarly, do not drink rainwater collected from a wooden roof that has been treated with some (possibly toxic) fire preventative or wood preservative.

An important principle in house construction is to so site the house that water drains away from it. This helps to ensure a dry basement and a firm foundation.

GOOD DRAINAGE

BAD DRAINAGE

Gutters help this. But by allowing rain to run off the roof all around the house you are effectively filling the area next to the foundation full of water. In areas of freezing weather, all this excess water in the ground can become a powerful force when it turns to ice working against the foundation with enormous pressure.

Each house's roof design will dictate the gutter layout, but the essentials always remain the same: provide gutters large enough to contain the rain from the area served; provide sufficient slope to the gutters to avoid standing water which will rust out or rot out (depending on whether you have metal or wooden gutters) your gutters; and ensure that you have adequate and efficient downspouts to lead the water away from the house (or into a collecting receptacle such as a storage tank or a rain barrel).

So after the snow is gone, but before the rains come, is the time to check the working condition of your gutters. Firstly, make sure that the whole system is connected — lengths may have become separated and downspouts may have broken loose.

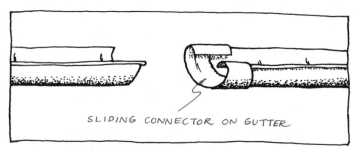

SLIDING CONNECTOR ON GUTTER

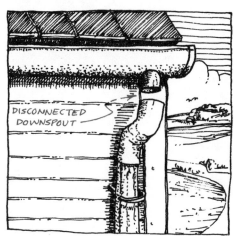

DISCONNECTED DOWNSPOUT

Secondly, make sure that there are no obstructions such as dams in the gutter or blockages in the downspout. The gutter entrances to downspouts are usually protected by wire baskets or strainers designed to prevent leaves etc., from washing into the downspout, but they often act as effective foundations for leaf dams, and can eventually rust away and collapse — in which case they should be replaced.

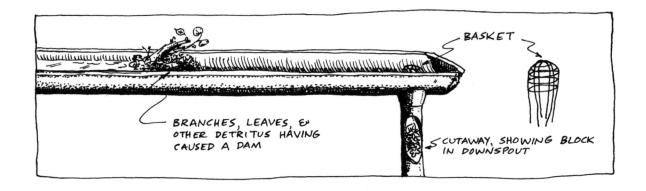

BASKET

BRANCHES, LEAVES, &
OTHER DETRITUS HAVING
CAUSED A DAM

CUTAWAY, SHOWING BLOCK
IN DOWNSPOUT

Thirdly, check that the gutters are sloped correctly and sufficiently ($\frac{1}{2}$" per 8' or 12 mm per 2$\frac{1}{2}$ m is generally enough). This may entail readjusting some of the gutter supports or hangers. Note that very long runs of gutter sometimes drain at both ends and consequently slope two ways.

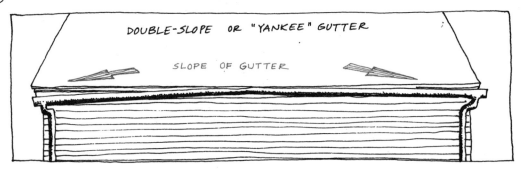

DOUBLE-SLOPE OR "YANKEE" GUTTER

SLOPE OF GUTTER

Lastly, check that there are no holes in the system caused by standing water having rusted out a section. If the system is still basically intact, but shows signs of rust, scrape the rust away and paint the gutters, inside and out, with special rustproofing paint. This will be a lot easier and cheaper than ignoring the rust and eventually having to replace the entire system.

H onses with wooden gutters, and gutters that are built into the eaves, ought to be inspected more assiduously than houses with attached metal gutters since repair or replacement of these types is that much more expensive.

SECTION OF REDWOOD GUTTER

HOUSE WITH GUTTERS IN EAVES ⇨

SITE DRAINAGE

This serious-sounding term simply means checking the immediate vicinity of the building to see if everything is still in place, literally! Every house should have an underground system of drainage included around the foundation to lead water away from the house. If it doesn't, or if the effectiveness of such a system should become impaired, a number of unpleasant things can happen, such as finding yourself surrounded by a moat or a marsh — which in freezing weather can expand and cause the ground to heave, damaging underground pipes and wires, destroying paths and steps, pushing plants out of the ground, and even causing foundations to collapse.

CRACKED PATH
TILTING OIL TANK
POOL OF WATER

The perfect situation for a house is on a dry, well-drained emminence (as illustrated on page 54), but not all houses are so situated; more often than not a house is on some kind of slope, which situation provides a built-in drainage problem on at least one side of the house. Even more problematical is a house built in a depression. Nevertheless, wherever it may be, it should have been the builder's duty to provide an adequate drainage system.

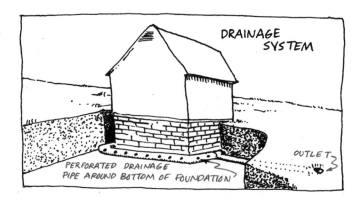

DRAINAGE SYSTEM

OUTLET

PERFORATED DRAINAGE PIPE AROUND BOTTOM OF FOUNDATION

A drainage system, by virtue of its location (buried next to the foundation), is difficult to service; indeed, if it fails the only cure may involve excavation and replacement. It is important therefore to keep an eye on conditions in this area and know how to recognize symptoms of incipient breakdown.

Assuming that such a system exists, you should not have pools of standing water next to the house after heavy rains or the spring melting of winter's snow.

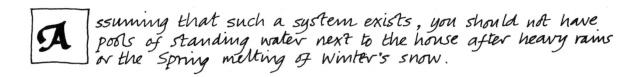

A common problem is the infiltration and blocking of the drainage pipes or tiles around the house by the roots of neighboring trees. Some species, allowed to grow too close to the house, are worse than others. Maples, for example, are infamous culprits, and seem to make a point of seeking out drainage pipes as a perfect water supply for their thirst, and consequently care should be taken when planting trees. Remember that the root system of the mature tree is as extensive as its crown.

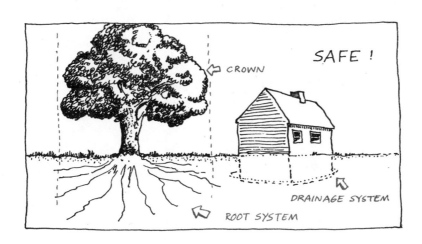

A nother cause of problems is that when the ground is not sloped away from the house sufficiently a catchment basin is formed. Waterlogged ground freezes faster than well-drained ground, and once frozen traps more water (which cannot seep down to the drainage tiles below), and the problem is compounded.

ou may have to grade the earth away from the house, provide a secondary drainage tile near the surface, or even dig a small ditch to carry away surface water.

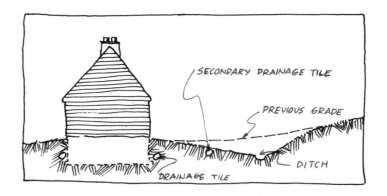

SECONDARY DRAINAGE TILE

PREVIOUS GRADE

DITCH

DRAINAGE TILE

 et another solution to an area that doesn't drain and which is either too wet or which heaves badly in cold weather, is to add a porch to that side of the house, so that the problem area simply doesn't get as wet.

 ne last thing to inspect is whether the water from the gutters and downspouts is being properly led away or whether it is adding to the problem.

7 f you do find a problem that requires a solution as major as excavation, it might be more convenient to delay taking care of it until the drier months of Summer — but bear in mind that it is sometimes difficult to recall how serious a problem was when some time has passed and all the symptoms have (temporarily) disappeared.

CULVERTS AND DITCHES
Related to site drainage is the job of checking,

after the snows have gone, that all your culverts and ditches running around the house, or under and along driveways, are still intact and clear in readiness for any heavy rains.

7 n areas of heavy snowfall, where snow plowing is necessary, culverts and ditches can suffer many mishaps which pass unnoticed until, in the middle of a rainstorm, you notice you are involved in a flood — or that part of your driveway is washing away.

T ake a quick walk around, carrying a long-handled shovel, and make sure the waterways are clear, and that part of the driveway didn't get plowed into a drainage ditch, or that when someone's car slid off the ice and into the bushes, the culvert entrance didn't become blocked.

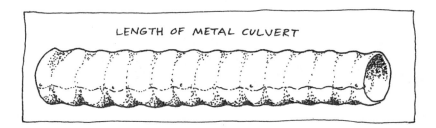

LENGTH OF METAL CULVERT

P oke around inside the culverts from time to time to see how rusty they have become. They are made to last a very long time but they can eventually collapse, and it is much more convenient if you can schedule replacement to suit your timetable rather than have your driveway collapse unexpectedly one day.

W hen you are sure the last snow has come and gone then it is time to rake back the driveway gravel from where it has been snow-plowed onto the lawn, and remove any posts you may have planted to help the plow locate the driveway (see NOVEMBER).

TANKS Many houses, individually situated, have their own supplies of cooking and heating gas, fuel oil, and sometimes, large water-supply tanks. It is a good idea, at this time of year, to check the installation of any of these tanks you may have, to see whether or not the Winter may have caused any shift in position which could cause a ruptured supply line. If frost or ground heaving is severe it may be advisable to reposition the tanks more securely — but, if possible, wait until all the frost and damp is out of the ground and the tanks are as empty as possible. For further tank maintenance see OCTOBER.

THINGS TO CHECK	YEAR										
DRIVEWAY for cracks, puddles, & potholes											
CULVERTS for sufficiency											
WALLS & FENCES for condition and placement											
BASEMENT VENT open											
BASEMENT for masonry decay, wood rot, & insect damage											

ANNUAL CHECKLIST OF HOME REPAIR FOR **APRIL**

A P R I L

ON DRIVEWAYS &
FENCES ·
ON FOUNDATIONS
& BASEMENTS :
MASONRY PROBLEMS,
ROT & DECAY,
INSECT DAMAGE ·

April in the country is the beginning of new life; the grass grows green again and you can smell the warmth seeping back into the earth. Even in the city April makes itself felt with warm spring rains that wash away Winter's grime. Indeed, April can be a very wet month, what with the ground thawing out, heavy rains, and little growth yet to absorb all the moisture.

However, if the culverts and ditches around your house were all checked out last month, you should suffer little if any damage, and instead can make notes on where to improve paths and driveways when the weather dries up.

DRIVEWAY

The time was when most houses were approached on foot up the garden path and entered through the front door, the horse or carriage presumably being left by the front gate. The advent of automobiles and busier roads has left the front doors of many older houses high and dry, blindly facing a busy highway on which it is no longer safe for horse or automobile to tarry. Nowadays, most houses have their main entrance oriented to the automobile's requirements, usually up a private driveway, whether it be a short suburban tarred strip or a longer, country shaled driveway.

W hether you have a short or a long driveway it will need a little attention from time to time. If it is a blacktop driveway check for cracks and incipient potholes, which can be easily repaired if attended to early enough with special tars readily available from hardware stores and lumberyards. If it is a longer driveway, made of shale, crushed stone, split rock, or gravel, it will require more careful attention if you want to make it last longer than a year or two.

Snow plowing exacts a heavy toll on these driveways by unavoidably removing large amounts of stone with the snow, but even more destructive is a hole or rut left to grow and eventually swallow large sections. No matter how carefully graded a new driveway may be it sooner or later develops ridges and depressions which begin to collect water. The holes seem to grow of their own accord; drivers attempt to skirt them and the driveway gradually changes from a smooth, straight run into a twisted and winding obstacle course. Much like a river, this is the natural development of a driveway, but the process can be slowed greatly by a little rake-work now and then.

When all the frost is out of the ground and Winter heaving has subsided and the ground is reasonably dry, fill in the holes and depressions with material raked from the high spots. If permanent ruts across the driveway seem bent on persisting, consider installing a new or additional culvert. It is difficult to force running water to go away; the best you can do is to provide it with a channel and try and keep it under control.

CULVERT

BETTER THIS ⬆   THAN THIS ⬆

A word of caution about culverts: the commonest mistake is to install something too small. Choose a culvert big enough to handle the maximum flow expected — even if this occurs only once every five years, because if you don't, this once-in-five-years flow could destroy the driveway, costing much more than the price of a larger culvert.

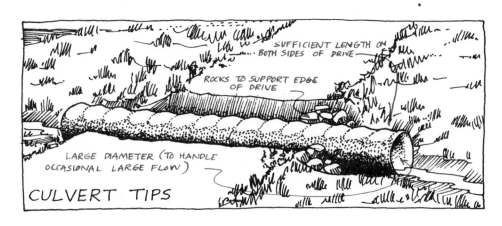

SUFFICIENT LENGTH ON BOTH SIDES OF DRIVE

ROCKS TO SUPPORT EDGE OF DRIVE

LARGE DIAMETER (TO HANDLE OCCASIONAL LARGE FLOW)

CULVERT TIPS

While it is important not to begin leveling your driveway until you are certain all the frost is gone and it has completely subsided, this is the best time of year to do this kind of work, especially more extensive repairs like major reshaping, since it allows the whole Summer for the driveway to be compacted firmly (by use), thereby minimizing the amount of loose surface material which snowplows are apt to scrape away.

Furthermore, if driveway repair has scarred your landscaping you can reseed now at a time when growth is fastest. Ground broken in the Autumn is more likely to remain bare over the Winter — leaching out valuable minerals and becoming subject to erosion.

While you've outside inspecting the driveway, cast an eye on garden walls and fences. These too may have suffered damage in the Winter, and may be profitably repaired before summer growth overwhelms them. If a driveway wall or fence has been knocked down or run into, before repairing it consider whether or not it should be moved a little. Some useful driveway dimensions are shown below.

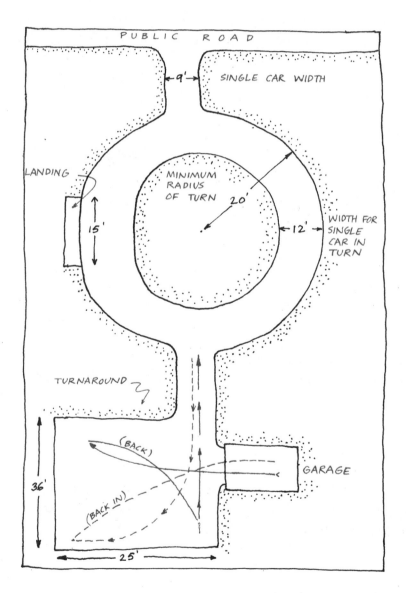

BASEMENTS

In April you should see that the basement vents are opened. These vents, which should have been closed at the beginning of the Winter (for a full discussion see OCTOBER), are one of the keys to keeping the basement or crawl space underneath your house dry and well ventilated — a condition whose importance is repeatedly demonstrated in the following section.

CLOSED   **BASEMENT VENT**   OPEN

FROM THE OUTSIDE   FROM THE INSIDE

Many of us never go downstairs to the cellar or basement, but it is worth the trip now and then, for a lot of trouble can start here and turn into some of the most expensive repair work it is possible for a house to need. The three main enemies against which you must remain on guard are discussed here in the following order:

MASONRY DETERIORATION
WOOD ROT AND DECAY
INSECT DAMAGE

Most houses have some form of masonry foundation, be it brick, stone, concrete, or concrete block. Properly built, masonry constructions are among the longest lasting of all human endeavors, but they can fail and you should know what to look for.

A little crumbling mortar and a few cracks, if not extensive, can be repaired and represent no major critical problem. In fact, if the house is old, some such is to be expected. But if all the mortar joints are soft or powdery to the touch you may have a problem with too much water on the outside of the foundation wall (for the cure of which see **MARCH**), or too much dampness inside the basement (for the cure of which see **JANUARY**), but in either case once the cause has been eliminated the joints should be cleaned out and recemented, a process known to masons as "pointing."

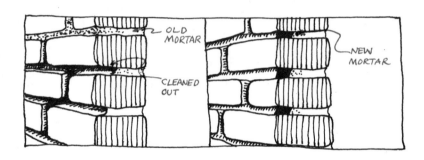

S mall cracks, especially hairline cracks in poured concrete, have little effect on the overall structure, but larger, extensive cracks that you can slip your little finger into can presage a bigger problem such as settling or excessive pressure on the outside of the foundation wall.

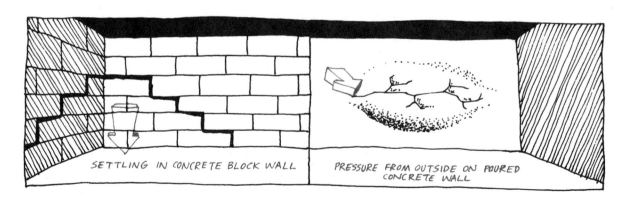

SETTLING IN CONCRETE BLOCK WALL   PRESSURE FROM OUTSIDE ON POURED CONCRETE WALL

These situations should be repaired as soon as possible for they represent not only a structural hazard but open the way (literally) to problems like water seepage and insect penetration. Sometimes all that is required is better drainage outside and some minor masonry repair inside; but it may prove necessary, especially if the ground has settled, to jack up that part of the house and replace the weakened section of foundation. This can become progressively more expensive the longer it is left, so catch it early by regular inspection at this time of the year – if you leave it until later the crack may close up and you will be unaware of the weakness.

Not only the perimeter walls, but all parts of the foundation, including piers and interior walls, should be checked for cracks, settling, and deterioration.

PIERS

Rot or decay is caused by tiny plants called fungi which can only live in wood which has a moisture content of at least thirty percent (and the warmer it is the faster they grow) – yet another reason for controlling the humidity of your house and especially the basement (for humidity see JANUARY).

Even so-called dry rot is caused by fungi which cannot survive without moisture — they manage by conducting moisture from wet areas to dry areas via structures called rhizomorphs. You should check all the wood structure in the basement for rot both by visual inspection — looking for soft, wet areas, and parts covered with fungus — and, since rot is not always evident on the surface, by probing with a sharp knife or other pointed instrument — if the wood is hard and resists the probe it is sound, but if it feels soft and mushy inside, decay is present.

If rot is discovered it is imperative to take immediate action, for it spreads and can cause ultimate collapse. You should perform surgery, excising the damaged wood and replacing it with sound wood, preferably treated with preservative, and ensure that the cause is eliminated.

THREE COMMON WOOD PRESERVATIVES

A word about preservatives: many are toxic and give off harmful vapors, which limits their use indoors, although some people periodically treat outside structures with creosote not only to preserve wood but to keep the insects away. They are really only effective to wood that is in contact with the ground if applied under pressure. Soaking provides less protection and simply painting on, even less. They can also cause paint to peel. The best way to preserve wood is to avoid contact with the ground and keep it dry!

There are various insects which can damage houses, among which are wood-destroying beetles, carpenter ants, and termites. By far the most dangerous are termites since their presence is often the least obvious. Termites, which feed on the wood from the inside, are most often seen on sunny Spring days when they swarm. They can be identified then by their two pairs of long wings which are of equal size — unlike winged ants, whose two pairs of wings are of unequal size. Without wings the difference is observable in the termite's thick waist and the ant's slender waist.

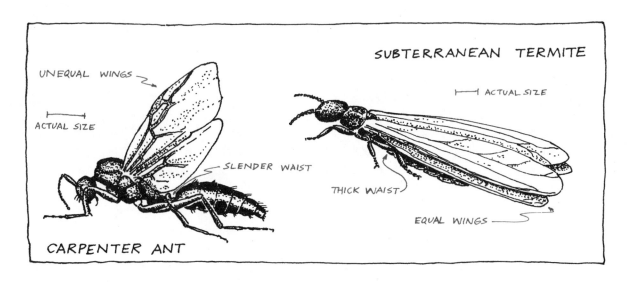

UNEQUAL WINGS

ACTUAL SIZE

SLENDER WAIST

CARPENTER ANT

SUBTERRANEAN TERMITE

ACTUAL SIZE

THICK WAIST

EQUAL WINGS

Other signs of termite presence are discarded wings underneath doors and windows and light fixtures, to which they are attracted when swarming, and the characteristic shelter tubes. These are little tubes of earth, which can be seen on masonry walls, enabling the termites to travel from the earth to the wood.

If you so much as suspect the presence of termites, call the exterminators at once!

C arpenter ants can be detected by telltale piles of sawdust. Unlike termites, which eat the wood, carpenter ants merely excavate it for living quarters, but the end result is the same — honeycombed wood, disastrously weakened from within. The ants also are more visible. Prevention is the best remedy — keep the basement dry and well ventilated, avoid piles of rotting wood near the house since these can harbor nests, and inspect regularly. If you do discover ants, do not panic, just patiently follow them until you find the nest (usually outside somewhere) and then destroy it and seal the entrance to the house they have been using — typically around porches, steps, and where the wood meets the foundation.

B eetles can be detected by small holes in the woodwork and powdery deposits around the holes. Beetles come and go, and since treatment is expensive, before you spend large sums of money make an easy test to see if your infestation is still active. Wipe away the powdery deposits and wait a few days to see if new powder, and holes, appear.

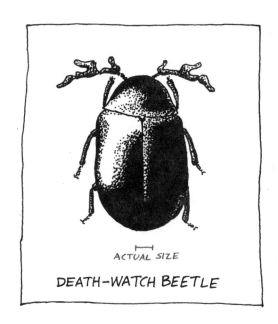

ACTUAL SIZE

DEATH–WATCH BEETLE

The prevention of beetles is the same as for other insects— keep the wood dry and well ventilated. Since serious infestations may require fumigation of the whole house, which is very expensive and dangerous, it is very important to be on the lookout for those small round or oval holes. Just a few may be brushed with insecticide. Furniture is sometimes treated by injecting insecticide into the beetle's exit holes with a syringe.

Against all these pests the best defence is a dry, well-ventilated basement, a thorough inspection at least once a year, and for complete, worry-free security a contract with a pest-control firm. They will treat your foundation with insecticide and perform annual inspections as well as eradicating any insect population you may discover.

THINGS TO CHECK	YEAR									
SEPTIC SYSTEM DRAIN FIELD for bogginess & smell										
BASEMENT for flooding or standing water										
SUMP PUMP for efficient operation										
ROOF for exterior damage & condition										
ATTIC LOUVERS for condition of screens										
ATTIC INSULATION for completeness										
SCREENS for holes, rents, & tears										

ANNUAL CHECKLIST OF HOME REPAIR FOR MAY

THE SEPTIC SYSTEM ·
BASEMENT FLOODING ·
THE ROOF & ATTIC ·
SCREENS ·

MAY

M ay is the month when people with gardens are involved in trying to outguess Mother Nature — will it freeze one more time or not? — for in most areas May is the month for planting. However, it is not just a question of waiting until all danger of frost is past but of also waiting for the ground to dry out enough so that it can be worked. If, indeed, it has been a wet Spring then now is a good time to check the following items around the house:

SEPTIC SYSTEM SUFFICIENCY
BASEMENT FLOODING

SEPTIC SYSTEM

If your house's plumbing wastes are absorbed by municipal sewers then you don't have to bother with this, but if you have your own septic system very wet weather is the time to check the efficiency of the drain field part of the system. Ideally, the waste goes into the septic tank, where bacteria break down the solids, leaving water to flow out into a drain field — also called a leaching field — which consists of perforated pipe laid in beds of gravel beneath the ground.

SEPTIC TANK   PERFORATED PIPE   DRAIN FIELD   GRAVEL

The size and composition of the leaching field should be sufficient to absorb the waste water without turning the area into a marsh. But if the ground is not porous enough, if the field is too small, or the pipes are clogged up, heavy rain will overload the system (if it is not already overloaded), and the resulting boggy area will tell you that improvements are needed—possibly additional lengths of drainage pipe.

DRAIN FIELD EXTEN-SION

PERFORATED DRAINAGE PIPE

GRAVEL IN TRENCH

If the boggy area also smells of sewage then you may have an additional problem. So long as the septic tank is large enough for the house and household and working well it should need no attention (and will not smell), but if it becomes overloaded or too much non-biodegradable detergent kills the bacteria (which break down the solid waste), then it will have to be pumped out. This procedure can be avoided, however, if you are careful to use only biodegradable detergents and help the bacteria by actually feeding them with a spoonful or two of yeast once in a while — just flush it down the toilet.

There are other ways to bypass the problem altogether which are more applicable when building a new house, but in the event your system becomes hopelessly incapacitated they deserve mention.

Firstly, toilets do not need to be connected to a septic tank (although in some localities old-fashioned building codes still insist on it) — there are toilets which perform their own composting operation in self-contained tanks, usually kept in the basement, and which need only be emptied once a year — at which time all you take out is odorless garden compost! Not only ecologically beneficial, these composting toilets greatly reduce the use of the septic tank and dramatically reduce your water consumption since they do not use any!

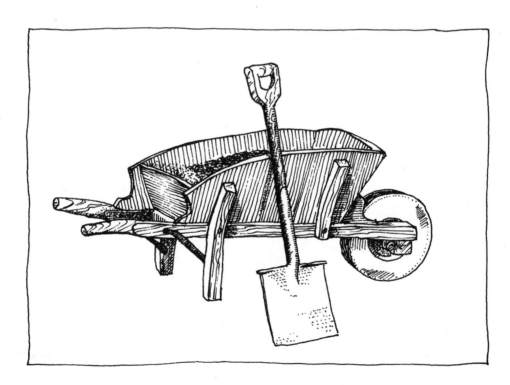

Secondly, many people use two separate septic tanks: one for "solid waste" and the other for "grey water." Grey water is water from dishwashers, washing machines, and showers and tubs. By keeping these separate, the grey water, which does not contain solid wastes needing to be broken down, may be leached off without overloading the main septic tank.

BASEMENT

Periods of heavy rain very often cause flooding in the basements of houses in low-lying or poorly drained areas. A damp basement is bad enough (see **APRIL**), but a flooded one can be disastrous, especially if the basement were to fill with water and cover the fuse box — in which case you should interrupt the power supply outside the house (by calling the power company if necessary).

Take a look downstairs after heavy rains to see if all is dry — if not you should install a sump pump. This is a pump which is located in the lowest part of the basement and to which all other areas should drain. The pump is automatically activated by water, which it then discharges outside the house. Ideally, the basement should be constructed to be waterproof, with bituminous seals and waterproof cement, etc., but many old houses are impossible to waterproof, being built with dry stone foundations on bare earth. In this case you should at least prevent flooding or standing water, and ensure adequate ventilation.

A t the same time as you are making the subterranean rounds of your house, checking for water, check also that any area or basement vents (see illustration on page 71) that may have been blocked or covered up during the Winter are open. The general rule for providing sufficient ventilation to basements or crawl spaces is one vent in every corner or one vent for every eight feet of perimeter, whichever is less.

ROOF

May is a good time of year to check the condition of the roof, and, if you have one, the attic, since it is not as likely to be as uncomfortable up here now as it is likely to be in mid-Summer or mid-Winter.

L eaks are an obvious sign that something is wrong, and a quick visual check of the condition of the roof covering is the first step in curing them. This should not have to be an annual inspection since asphalt shingles can be expected to

last for fifteen years at least, cedar shakes for twenty, and slate and tin roofs for much, much longer, but take a look anyway to see if anything has blown away, or if branches of overhanging trees may have fallen and caused any damage, or if there appears to be any damage to any of the flashing (the metal seam around chimneys and at the junction of different roof slopes).

R emember that a leak inside the house may have traveled some distance down a rafter before appearing on the ceiling, so do not look for its origin and cause only around the area of its appearance.

I f your roof is covered with asphalt shingles, they should not be flaking or cracked, and should still possess a good covering of surface granules. If they look bald and are rounded at the edges get ready to schedule a roofing job, for a defective roof can lead to many other problems if left unrepaired.

Next, look inside the roof. Most houses have some attic, and this is usually an uninsulated space above the upper rooms, within the roof structure. The most important thing up here is that this area be well ventilated to prevent the potentially damaging effects of condensation. The commonest situation is for an attic to be built with louvered vents at each end, in the gables.

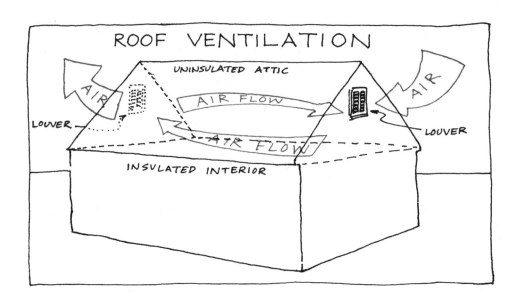

ROOF VENTILATION

UNINSULATED ATTIC

AIR

AIR FLOW

AIR

LOUVER

AIR FLOW

LOUVER

INSULATED INTERIOR

If you go up into the attic on a sunny, but still cold day — when the temperature is down around freezing — and that side of the roof which faces away from the sun is damp or wet, then there is not enough ventilation and you should install more openings, or possibly a fan to push the air around. Of course, if the warmed area of the house is properly furnished with vapor barriers (see **JANUARY**), there shouldn't be that much moisture to condense up here anyway, but if there is, more ventilation will help.

N ow one thing leads to another, and a hole in the gable to allow ventilation will also attract unwanted tenants in the form of birds, bats, rodents, and insects. The vents therefor should be screened, and this screening should be checked once a year. Firstly, it can become torn and present no barrier to anything wanting to make a home in your attic, and secondly it can get clogged up with leaves and grime and allow no air to pass, effectively sending you back to square one in the ventilation game. So brush it clean, and patch any holes, or replace it if this is easier.

ATTIC   CEILING JOIST   TUNNELS & NESTS   INSULATION

W hile you are doing this, check that you still have a continuous blanket of insulation between the ceiling joists that form the floor of the attic, because sometimes little rodents will chew away tunnels and nests, thereby creating heat leaks for you. If this has happened, get a cat or set some traps, and replace the missing insulation — usually just rearranging it is all that is necessary.

SCREENS As the weather turns warmer you will be wanting to open the windows to ventilate yourself. It can be bad enough in the daytime with flies, bluebottles, and bumblebees buzzing around inside but at night, if you leave the window open and a light on you can be overwhelmed by clouds of moths and junebugs, and eaten alive by swarms of midges, gnats, and mosquitoes. Screens are not only a luxury for a closed-in porch or veranda, but in many areas a virtual necessity for the house itself. Now, then, is the time to install your screens.

 s you take down and store away the storm windows, make sure each unit is marked so that you know exactly where it goes when it comes time to put them in again.

NUMBERED PINS

 efore you put up the screens look them over carefully for tears or holes, for they are easier to repair before being installed. What sometimes may at first glance appear to be a small hole is actually just the mesh spread apart. A nail or some other sharp object can be used to realign the wires. Real tears can be repaired by gluing or weaving – but both look like patches, and if the tear is large and appearances are very important, the only solution is to replace the whole screen wire.

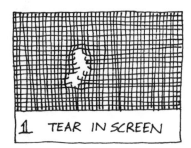

1 TEAR IN SCREEN

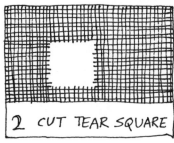

2 CUT TEAR SQUARE

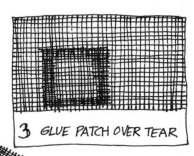

3 GLUE PATCH OVER TEAR

2a CUT LARGER SQUARE PATCH

This is a good technique for wire or nylon-mesh screens, and epoxy is a good glue to use, but even shellac will work. For a more permanent job on wire-mesh screens, the weaving method shown below is best.

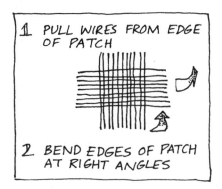

1 PULL WIRES FROM EDGE OF PATCH

2 BEND EDGES OF PATCH AT RIGHT ANGLES

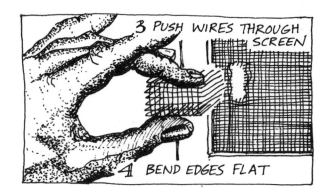

3 PUSH WIRES THROUGH SCREEN

4 BEND EDGES FLAT

THINGS TO CHECK	YEAR									
LIGHTNING RODS & CONDUCTORS for presence & connection										
CONCRETE for cracks & chips										
BRICKWORK for efflorescence & spalling										
STUCCO for cracks & holes										

ANNUAL CHECKLIST OF HOME REPAIR FOR JUNE

J U N E

LIGHTNING
PROTECTION ·
· MASONRY REPAIRS :
CRACKS,   BROKEN
CONCRETE,
EFFLORESCENCE,
SPALLING,
STUCCO DEFECTS ·

JUNE

June, by our calendar, the sixth month, is halfway through the year and the official beginning of Summer, and yet in apparent contradiction this is the month when the days begin to get shorter. But then Nature never did wait for Man or pay any heed to his arbitrary decisions. The most that Man can do is to try and protect himself against Nature's periodic outbursts of violence, such as volcanic eruptions, earthquakes, storms, and lightning. It is this last with which we are presently concerned since June marks the onset of the Summer thunderstorm season.

LIGHTNING PROTECTION

Lightning is the result of large quantities of positive (or negative) electrical charges building up in storm clouds and being attracted to an equal quantity of negative (or positive) charges in the ground below. When the attraction becomes great enough the gap is suddenly bridged, releasing enormous amounts of energy (millions of volts and thousands of amperes). Nearby air molecules are heated up and explode — which causes the noise we call thunder.

The important thing to bear in mind is that the bridging effect takes place at the point where the two charges can get closest to one another, that is, from the top of the tallest objects in the area of the build up, whether these be trees, poles, masts of ships, or, from what is of concern to us here, houses. The damage that can ensue from this sudden passage of enormous energy is caused by the resistance of the path taken by the "spark." For example, wood is not a very good conductor of electricity and so, resisting it, gets rather badly damaged. Copper rods or wires on the other hand are very good conductors of electricity, which means they offer little resistance and consequently suffer minimal damage.

If, therefore, your house stands out in an open area it should be protected from a possible lightning strike by a system of terminals or rods which, projecting above the roof, are connected by means of heavy cables to one another and then to equally thick wires leading to metal plates, rods, or pipes buried deep in the ground.

For maximum protection and insurance benefits, such a system should be installed by professional installers and supplied with a Master Label plate certifying that sufficient Underwriters' Laboratory - approved rods, conductors, and grounds have been satisfactorily installed.

JUNE

Not only the house but television or radio antennas, water pipes, waste pipes, and wiring systems too should be equipped with suitable lightning arrestors. And if you care about especially tall and exposed trees, these too should be protected by lightning rods. The maintenance of these systems consists of making sure that all the constituent parts are still in place and connected.

MASONRY REPAIRS

June is an ideal month to inspect and take care of your masonry. There is quite a lot of masonry in an average home, even in a predominantly wooden house, but its care and repair is the same no matter whether it is part of the foundation, a walk or driveway, steps, patios, brick walls, block walls, stuccoed walls, or concrete block piers.

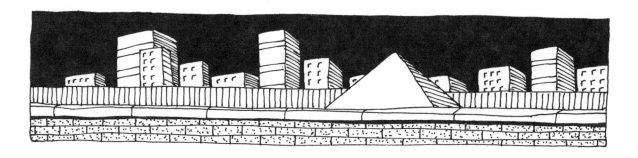

Although concrete is generally thought of as relatively indestructible, it can nevertheless suffer deterioration and even collapse. It can develop cracks, as a result of settling foundations or excessive drying, and in temperate regions freezing weather can enlarge these cracks to destructive proportions. Rain or dampness can also take their toll, resulting in conditions known by the ominous terms of efflorescence and spalling!

o be efficient you should make a checklist of all the masonry parts in and around your home and perform an annual inspection looking for the following defects:

CRACKS, HAIRLINE OR EXTENSIVE

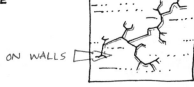 ON WALLS

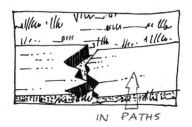 IN PATHS

BROKEN OR CHIPPED AREAS

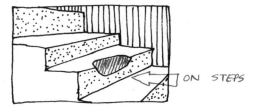 ON STEPS

EFFLORESCENCE

ON BRICK WALLS

SPALLING

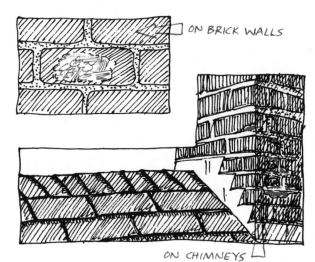

ON CHIMNEYS

STUCCO DEFECTS

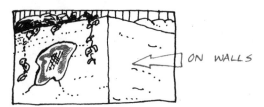 ON WALLS

JUNE

CRACKS Small hairline cracks are almost unavoidable on large rendered areas, such as a stuccoed wall, or smoothly cemented concrete walk, but if they appear too big to be hidden by a coat of paint they may be easily repaired with a variety of materials suitable to different situations.

It is really just a question of undercutting the crack, cleaning it out, wetting it, and patching it. The undercutting is done in order to prevent the patch from falling out, and may be done with a hardened-steel tool called a cold chisel. The cleaning out is accomplished with a stiff wire brush, in order to remove all loose particles and ensure a good bond.

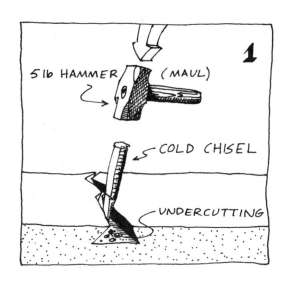

1

5 lb HAMMER (MAUL)

COLD CHISEL

UNDERCUTTING

2

WIRE BRUSH FOR CLEANING CRACK

3 WETTING CRACK

The third step consists of thoroughly wetting down the area which the new cement will contact in order to prevent the existing material from drawing the moisture from the new before it has had time to set properly. You do not want to leave puddles of water, however. As a further guarantee of a good bond between the old and new work, various latex bonding agents can be applied to the crack now.

F inally, the crack may be filled either with cement you have mixed yourself — one part Portland cement to three parts sand, and not so much water that the mix is sloppy, but not so little that the mix is too stiff to work (if you can throw it against the wall and it sticks there, it is just right) — or with a commercial masonry patching material such as a latex, epoxy, vinyl, or acrylic cement that comes in a cartridge. If there is only a small amount to be done and you prefer to use cement, which is still considered the best material, you may find it more convenient to buy a pre-mixed bag — they are available in different sizes from 10 lbs to 90 lbs.

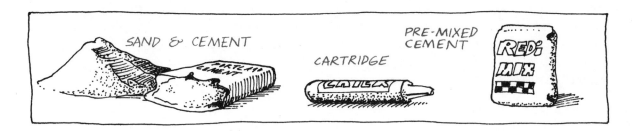

SAND & CEMENT   PRE-MIXED CEMENT   CARTRIDGE

1 n any event, work the material of your choice well into the crack, removing all air bubbles, and then keep it damp — by covering it with plastic and wetting it down occasionally for the first forty-eight hours. If it dries too quickly it will only crack again and you will be back where you started!

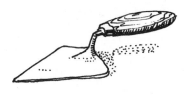

7 f the crack you want to repair is wide, deep, or the two sides of it are uneven, the procedure is basically the same as for smaller cracks except that in the case of flat surfaces such as paths or walkways you may want to try and elevate the sunken side and keep it level by packing sand underneath.

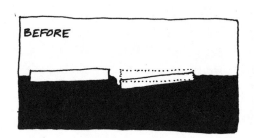
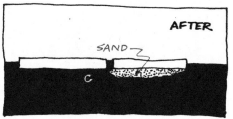

W henever severe cracks appear and the surface becomes very uneven it is wise to ascertain the cause of the problem, which may be something like poor drainage (see MARCH) and then correct it before effecting any repairs. Concrete paths especially can deteriorate very rapidly if not properly drained or poorly founded in areas of freezing weather. There is little that can be done, however, about the problem of subsidence or fault-related earth movements.

BROKEN CONCRETE

The procedure for repairing larger holes and damage in concrete, such as the broken edges of concrete steps, is similar to the process of repairing cracks. Provide a flat "landing" for the patching material by chipping away with a cold chisel, and dampen the area, and then fill it — providing some support for the wet mix — which should contain some small stones (the stones are the extra ingredient that turns cement into concrete).

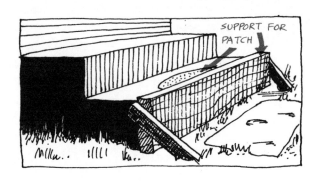

The support, which should be greased so that concrete will not stick to it when it's removed, must be very firmly held in place because wet concrete is very heavy. Just as when repairing a crack, it is of paramount importance to allow the repair to cure slowly (or it _will_ crack) by keeping it damp and covered to start with. Depending on the weather and the thickness of the new work, it can take up to a week to cure or harden completely. So if in doubt, be patient.

EFFLORESCENCE

Sometimes mineral salts contained in bricks, especially new bricks, are pushed to the surface by moisture; this often unsightly effect is known as efflorescence. It can be removed by a vigorous cleaning of the bricks with a wire brush and a solution of one part muriatic acid and four parts water. Muriatic acid is very strong and very dangerous stuff so be careful. Continued efflorescence is best cured by eliminating the source of the moisture, for it can be amazing how many times you can clean the bricks only to have more salts pushed out.

SPALLING

This unusual term comes from an old Scottish word used in quarries and stone-yards — spale — which means chip or splinter. Spalling describes the process of brickwork deterioration caused by bricks soaking up moisture and then flaking apart during freezing weather as the moisture turns to ice and expands. Bricks badly spalled are best removed altogether. Replacements, after having been mortared* into place, can be treated with a clear brick-sealant to prevent the condition reoccurring.

1 Chip out damaged brick (or bricks) with cold chisel.
2 Clean hole, dampen it thoroughly, and trowel in a bed of mortar.
3 Slide in new brick (or bricks) and pack mortar around sides.

* Mortar, which is cement with added lime, may also be bought in small, ready-mixed bags.

STUCCO DEFECTS

Stucco, which actually means any kind of plasterwork, is generally taken to refer to an outside covering of cement. Exterior walls are sometimes stuccoed with pebbledash — a mixture of cement and fine stones. Very often, a mortar pigment is added to give color. When this needs repair because of cracks or holes remember that it can be very difficult to match the original color and to achieve uniformity you may have to give the whole surface a new finish coat.

Cracks in stucco are repaired like cracks in concrete; chip away and undercut, clean out the crack, wet the area, and apply a finish coat. For holes you will have to effect the repair in stages. Stucco normally goes on in three coats; the first, or "scratch" coat is applied over chicken wire — and if the area you are repairing is damaged this deeply, you may have to repair the wire as well — and then allowed to dry for forty-eight hours. Before it dries completely, however, you must scratch the surface to provide for better adhesion of the second coat, hence the name "scratch" coat. The second coat should be allowed to dry for up to four days before applying the finish coat.

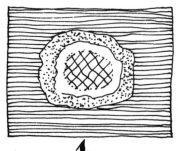

1

Repair chicken wire and apply scratch coat (white).

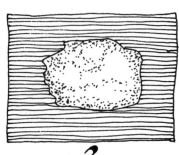

2

Let scratch coat dry and apply second coat (speckled).

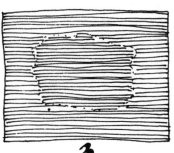

3

Let second coat dry and apply finish coat.

THINGS TO CHECK	YEAR										
HYGROMETER for excessive humidity											
METAL SIDING for rust or oxidation											
WOOD SIDING for rot & paint state											
SHINGLES for cracks, bulges & splits											
INTERIOR DECORATION for paint & plaster condition											
ATTICS & CUPBOARDS for pests & infestations											

ANNUAL CHECKLIST OF HOME REPAIR FOR JULY

J   U   L   Y

ON SIDING : WOOD,
METAL & SHINGLES.
INTERIOR DECORATION.
PESTS & OTHER GUESTS.

JULY

In the daye of Seynte Svythone : rane ginneth rininge
Forti dawes mid ywone : Cestez such tithinge

(If it rains on St. Swithin's day it will rain for forty more)
FROM A THIRTEENTH-CENTURY MANUSCRIPT AT EMMANUEL COLLEGE, CAMBRIDGE

July sees two days traditionally associated with rain : St. Swithin's day (July **15**th), and St. Margaret's day (July **20**th). July is also referred to as having patch-work-quilt weather — sun stitched with raindrops. Be that as it may, the humidity in July is generally greater than in Winter, and now is a good time to check that it is not excessive and having bad effects on your house and its contents. For a complete discussion of humidity, too much and too little, see JANUARY.

One tip for swollen doors or drawers (a result of high humidity) is worth remembering: although the cure is to reduce the moisture content of the article (by lowering the humidity), you can make the moving parts move more easily if you rub them with soap. Such a treatment is good preventive medicine even if wooden drawers are not sticky; it helps them slide more freely.

SIDING

Take a walk around the outside of your house and inspect the condition of the external skin or covering — the siding. This may be of different materials, each of which has its problems. Aside from brick or stucco, which was discussed in JUNE, there are three common types of siding:

> METAL
> WOOD — PAINTED OR UNPAINTED
> SHINGLES — WOOD OR ASBESTOS

METAL

Any iron or steel, such as bolt heads or various pieces of exterior hardware like shutter hinges or tension bolts, should, of course, be kept painted or they will rust away. If you should have any stainless steel or aluminum on the outside of your house it will only require an occasional washing with soap and water to keep it clean and looking new; a light coat of paste wax will help protect it. Copper, brass, and bronze must all be kept polished if you want them to remain shiny. While polishing is all right for things like brass doorknockers, copper roofs and flashing are usually left to tarnish and develop a prestigious antique green patina.

BRASS DOOR KNOB

BRASS KEY HOLE

BRASS LETTER BOX

BRASS KICK PLATE

The only metal commonly used for extensive exterior covering is aluminum, and since for this application it usually comes already painted, it needs little attention; indeed this is one of the few points in its favor. However, scratches and dents do occur and if you do have to paint, be sure to use a paint made expressly for metal surfaces. Unpainted aluminum surfaces take paint better if they are allowed to weather for a while first, and then given an undercoat of a zinc-chromate metal primer. For unpainted areas of aluminum trim, such as window frames, a periodic coating of liquid wax will help prevent the pitting and discoloration which can occur under certain atmospheric conditions.

WOOD

Wood is the commonest material used for the exterior covering of houses in America, and can be left untreated to weather, be finished with various preservatives, which may impart a stain or be clear, or be painted. Whatever is the case with your house, the first job is to look for damage not to the finish, but to the wood itself — a beautifully painted piece of rotten wood is still a piece of rotten wood.

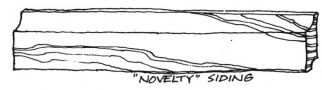

"NOVELTY" SIDING

C heck places where the wood comes into contact with concrete or cement, such as steps or porches. The construction should drain the water away from the wood or it will eventually rot. Check places where the wood comes into contact with the ground (never a good idea, and something to be changed if you find it). Another common fault is to find planters placed against the foundation and siding — with no ventilation space between, this is inviting decay. Check the areas around gutters and downspouts to make sure that the siding is not getting wet and everything is draining away properly. Check the joints between the siding and windows and doors to see that all is tightly caulked or filled. All these places are potentially subject to rot and decay. If you find any, the damaged wood must be removed and replaced. Check once a year and you will avoid expensive repairs and your paint job (if the siding is painted) will last longer.

a WATER ON PORCH
b SIDING TOUCHES GROUND
c PLANTER TOUCHES SIDING
d DOWNSPOUT BROKEN
e GAP BETWEEN DOOR & SIDING

N ow look at the paint. How it wears can tell you a lot about the condition of your house and whether you simply need to repaint or make some structural changes. Exterior paint is designed to shed water — from the outside — but if because of defective caulking, leaky gutters (see **MARCH**), corroded flashing (see **MAY**), or poor vapor barriers (see **JANUARY**) inside the house, moisture is allowed to seep into the wall and soak the wood behind the paint, blisters, bubbles, and peeling will occur, no matter how much you paint and repaint. Therefore, whenever you notice any blisters, etc., check for all the possible causes mentioned above.

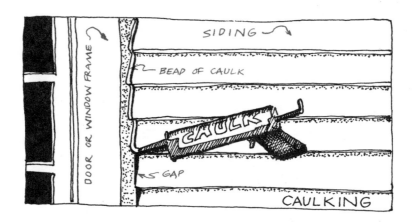

S ometimes all of the above seems to be in order and yet the paint still peels. In this case, small louvers inserted in the siding are often sufficient to ventilate the area behind the siding. One 1inch louver inserted in each closed-off area between the framing members, especially over windows, is usually enough. The framing members in newer houses are commonly 16 inches apart and can be located by the vertical rows of nails in the siding.

7 f only the top layer of paint has peeled – revealing the old paint underneath – then this indicates that the newer paint was applied to a dirty or damp surface. Never paint unless the following conditions obtain: the temperature is between 50° and 90° Fahrenheit; the surface is dry and clean; the old peeling areas have been all scraped away; cracks and holes (including nailhead holes) have been caulked and filled; damaged or rotted wood has been replaced; and the paint you are about to use is applicable over the existing paint.

T his last is especially important for, without proper preparation, certain paints cannot be successfully applied over other types, for example, latex paints over oil paints, or oil paints over chalking paints. There is usually a way of using any paint you want, even if it means completely removing all the old paint, but it is very important to check up on the manufacturer's instructions. This is the kind of thing which is important to do if you are having someone else do the work, for house painting can be very expensive, and the wrong paint can waste a lot of money in a very short time.

SHINGLES

Wood or asbestos shingles used for siding should be inspected annually for splits, cracks, bulges, and missing pieces, for damage can ensue to the exposed sheathing and the inner wall. If the shingles are misaligned or bulging, the nails holding them may simply have worked loose, and all you have to do is to hammer them back in — or if they no longer hold, hammer in new ones — but be sure to use galvanized, ringed nails which grip well and do not rust. Drill a pilot hole first to avoid splitting the shingle and avoid hitting the shingle itself for they tend to crack easily.

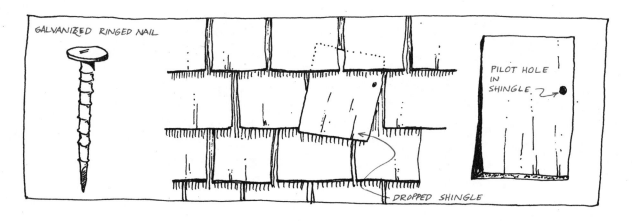

GALVANIZED RINGED NAIL

PILOT HOLE IN SHINGLE

DROPPED SHINGLE

Cracked shingles do not need to be replaced but should have a piece of waterproof building paper slipped up behind the crack or split and secured by a galvanized nail through the butt (the lower or thicker end) of the shingle.

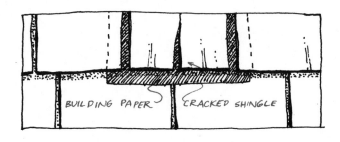

BUILDING PAPER   CRACKED SHINGLE

M ore seriously damaged shingles should be removed and then replaced by new ones. The damaged shingle itself may be further fragmented in order to remove all the pieces, but especial care must be taken to remove the nails that were holding it in place, or you will not be able to insert the new shingle.

 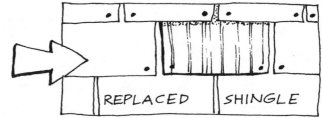

REPLACED SHINGLE

T he nails holding asbestos shingles are generally visible and can be chiseled or sawn off or drilled out as shown below.

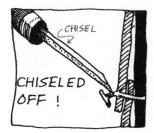  

CHISELED OFF !

SAWN OFF !

HACKSAW BLADE

DRILLED OUT!

T he nails holding wood shingles are generally nailed through the top of the shingle and are consequently hidden by the shingle above. Although they are a little more difficult to remove, it can generally be done by sliding a hacksaw blade up under the shingle to be removed and sawing through the back of the nail.

INTERIOR DECORATION

In the same way that the previous section could have been called the "out" siding, this section could well be called the "in" siding. This is not, however, the place to give detailed instructions on interior decorating, but an annual check on the condition of wallpaper and plaster should be made.

J f redecorating is to be considered, it is often most convenient to schedule it for this time of year when windows and doors can be left open while paint is drying. While inspecting the walls and ceilings for shabby paint, etc., look also for signs of more serious damage such as water stains, indicating a leaky roof (see **MAY**), or badly cracked plaster, indicating foundation settling (see **APRIL**).

PESTS

Mention has already been made of the little rodents that sometimes inhabit the insulation in the attic (see **MAY**), but there are various other creatures, large and small, that from time to time may demonstrate a desire to share your home with you, and who, indeed, in some instances may appear to be making a concerted effort to actually evict you and take over completely. Any such serious threat should be met with prompt retaliation; it is after all your spot on earth, and you have a right to defend it against the ultimate destruction that certain invaders would foolishly bring about, even to their own disadvantage.

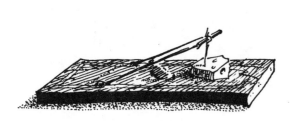

Such invasions include termites, carpenter ants, and wood-boring beetles (see **MAY**). However, many other creatures deserve more of a compromise for they may actually be useful. For example, a couple of bats in the attic are all right since they help keep the wasps under control, and wasps in moderation are not all bad since they help keep the spiders down, which in turn are very useful in reducing the fly population. Since in practice it is very difficult to completely secure a house against every invader, a balanced population is actually to be encouraged.

Cats, unless you overfeed them and tie them down, can generally be relied on to keep the rats and mice away. If you live in the country, a dog will keep the raccoons out of your chicken house and away from your garbage cans. Deer and rabbits in your garden can only be kept out by tall fences which also go somewhere underground to thwart burrowers.

Skunks and porcupines, which occasionally take up residence underneath houses (porcupines especially like to chew away porch supports), are best caught in humane traps, given a stern lecture, and removed to another neighborhood — do not let the dog attempt to see them off the property or you will end up with a stinky house or a spiky dog — or both.

If things like silverfish, cockroaches, millipedes, and salamanders start appearing out of cupboards then your house is too damp — air it all out and keep all the hidden spaces clean — this is much better than poisoning your house with various insecticides.

It is said that no matter how much you clean there will always be at least one spider in every bedroom. One is all right with me, especially if it is discreet, but sometimes things arrive in droves (or swarms, or herds, or whatever) for no apparent reason. Try and identify the newcomers before you take action. Ladybugs (or ladybirds as they are more prettily called in England) which often hibernate under shingles sometimes come out to bask in a warm winter's sun, and their numbers can be staggering. But do not rush for the exterminator, they are our best allies in combating that pernicious menace — the aphid.

Elm-leaf beetles, on the other hand, which also are wont to make sudden appearances "en masse" in the Autumn, should be swept up and eliminated since they do little that is good and help carry the fungal disease that has decimated elm trees.

Screens and a clean, well-ventilated house are your best protection. Specific deterrents and remedies are as legion as the pests they are designed for, but the most important rule is to try and not go overboard in combating one particular enemy, for everything is interconnected, and you cannot remove one part without affecting the remainder, often producing a worse problem (for yourself) than you had at first.

THINGS TO CHECK	YEAR									
PRESSURE TANK for leaks & correct pressure										
WELL for quality & quantity of water										
HOT WATER HEATER for sediment, temperature, & leaks										
PLUMBING FIXTURES for leaks & blockages										
VENT STACK for blockages										

ANNUAL CHECKLIST OF HOME REPAIR FOR AUGUST

WELLS ·
PRESSURE TANKS ·
HOT WATER HEATERS ·
PLUMBING FIXTURES ·
VENT STACK ·

AUGUST

Almost every year sees the breaking of one weather record or another – the most snow since **1859**, the latest frost since **1902**, the driest Summer in living memory. Since some aspect of the weather always seems to be demonstrating one extreme or another it is hard to understand how we ever arrive at any characterization of the seasons at all. The fact is though, that despite continual surprises, generalizations can be made about what weather to expect – just never for today!

So when you read this it will probably be the wettest Summer you have ever experienced, and yet in general it remains true to say that August is one of the drier months. It is for this reason that it is the best month to overhaul your water supply, because if it is adequate now it should be adequate throughout the rest of the year.

Similarly, drainage problems are best rectified now while the water level is at its lowest; new channels may be dug and culverts installed without having to deal with torrents of water rushing by.

AUGUST

WATER SUPPLY

Practically all urban homes use city water — the only thing that is important to know in this situation is where the stopcock or main gate valve is. This is the main supply control valve, the one you should turn off if you have any problem with leaks or burst pipes. It can sometimes be hard to find, but make sure you know where it is, even if you have to call in a plumber to help locate it, because it will be even harder to find it in an emergency.

Together with knowing how to turn off the electricity this is the most important thing to know about your house. You may not ever want to do any repairs at all yourself, but you __must__ know these two things or even a simple problem can turn into a major catastrophe.

Rural homes and many suburban homes have their own water supply and this should be checked once a year rather than being taken for granted — or you run the risk of losing it at the most inopportune moment.

Most likely the water will be pumped up from a well or drawn from a spring or stream. Unless the house is gravity fed (which means that the supply is sufficiently higher than the house for its own weight to cause it to run out of the faucets with enough pressure), there will be a pressure tank between the source and the house.

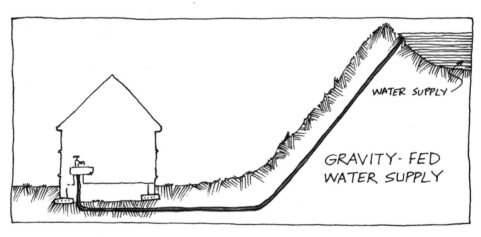

WATER SUPPLY

GRAVITY-FED WATER SUPPLY

PRESSURE TANK

WELL

WELL-PRESSURE TANK

AUGUST

The same paramount rule applies to houses with their own supply as does to houses with a municipal supply — know how to shut it off! If you have a pressure tank there will be two choices: you can shut off the water going into the tank or coming out of it. If you need to drain the whole house (because, for example, you are going away in Winter and intend to turn off the heat), then turn off the supply _before_ the pressure tank and drain everything, including the tank itself. If, on the other hand, it is just a question of working on one section of the plumbing in the house, use the valve controlling the flow coming _out_ of the pressure tank.

PRESSURE TANK

a This valve controls the flow into the tank. The pipe goes from the tank to the well, probably disappearing through the wall or into the floor.

b This valve controls the flow out of the tank. The pipe runs from the tank to the hot water heater and other pipes around the house.

c The pressure gauge.

d The reset button.

e The electricity switch.

AUGUST

It is also possible, of course, that you may be able to turn off the water closer to the involved section since many plumbing fixtures have their own shutoff valves — look under the bathroom sink, for example. Nevertheless, you should still know how to shut off the whole system at the main valve.

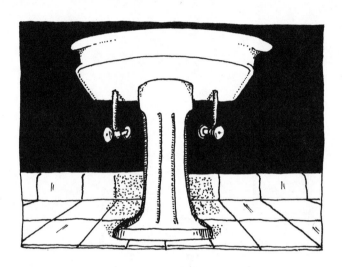

Once you know how to turn off the water supply, the next thing is to know how to turn it on again. If a pressure tank is involved this is not always simply a matter of turning the appropriate valve. The function of the pressure tank is twofold: to activate the well pump when required, and to supply water to the house at sufficient pressure. Various problems can arise as a result of too little pressure or too much pressure so it pays to become familiar with the readings on the gauge during normal conditions. The gauge is usually located somewhere on the tank and registers the pressure inside the tank in pounds per square inch (PSI).

When the pressure in the tank drops (because you have drawn off water somewhere in the system), a switch is activated that starts the well pump sending more water into the tank. When there is once again sufficient water in the tank the pressure will have risen enough to shut off the pump.

If the pump keeps running and the pressure does not rise you may have an empty well or a leak. Turn off the switch supplying electricity to the pump and call the plumber. You do not want the pump to run continuously or it will eventually burn out.

The opposite problem of how to start the pump is easier to deal with. Make sure the electricity is on and the valve is open and simply hold the reset button down for 15 or 20 seconds. The pump should start running, and continue to run after you release the button, and the pressure should rise to around 40 PSI and stay there after the pump stops. You then have a full tank.

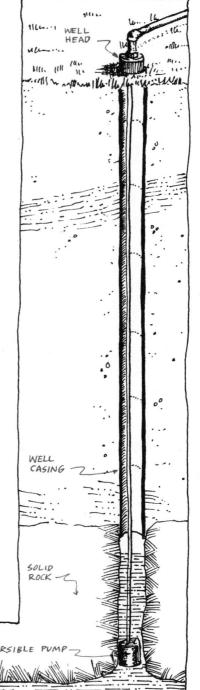

WELL HEAD

WELL CASING

SOLID ROCK

ANATOMY OF A WELL

SUBMERSIBLE PUMP

AUGUST

Armed with all this knowledge, your periodic check should consist of inspecting for leaks, making sure that the pump does not run continuously, and that the pressure gauge reads around **40** PSI. Also, in areas of freezing weather, the whole installation, from well head to pressure tank, should be well insulated.

To check the condition and efficiency of the well, run the water in the house for **20** minutes or so. The pump should go on and off, the pressure should hold steady, and the water should stay clear. If all this happens in August (typically the driest month), you have a good well. But if the water slows to a trickle or turns brown, you may not have enough. The other thing to check once in a while is the quality of the water. This should be done by letting the water run for a few minutes from a faucet that you have previously held a match under (to kill any bacteria in the spigot), and then taking a sample to your local health office where it can be analyzed for potability.

HOT WATER HEATER

A major part of a home's water system is the hot water heater. Unless you have hot water supplied from the central heating system or some kind of solar installation, your hot water will most likely be made in a separate tank run by electricity or gas. These appliances are among the most trouble-free in the house and require little mainte-nance.

New hot water heaters should be partly drained once a year (after turning off the electricity or gas as the case may be), to flush out any accumulated sediment. The drain valve is typically located near the bottom of the tank, and usually has provision for attaching a hose to it so that you can run off the water into a convenient drain. Simply open the drain valve and let the water run until it runs out clear. However, if you have an old tank, or have not performed this operation for a long time, beware! The valve may have frozen into position, and opening it may make it impossible to reseal it, and you could have a leak repairable only by replacement.

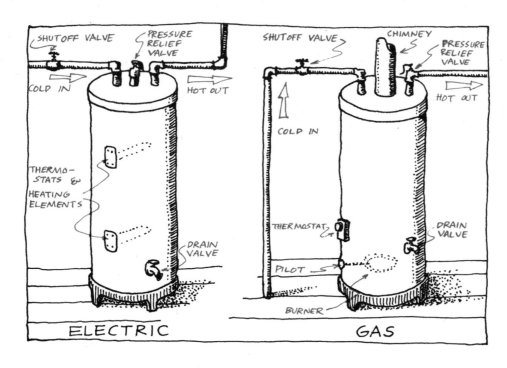

SHUTOFF VALVE   PRESSURE RELIEF VALVE   SHUTOFF VALVE   CHIMNEY   PRESSURE RELIEF VALVE

COLD IN   HOT OUT   COLD IN   HOT OUT

THERMO-STATS & HEATING ELEMENTS   THERMOSTAT   DRAIN VALVE

DRAIN VALVE   PILOT

BURNER

ELECTRIC   GAS

AUGUST

The hot water heater should also be checked for the correct thermostat setting. The lower the temperature of the water that comes out of the faucet, the cheaper it is to run the heater. If every time you run the hot water you have to run the cold water too, you are wasting money and energy. While gas hot water heaters have only one thermostat, it is important to remember that most electric hot water heaters have two, an upper and a lower. If you only adjust one you have achieved nothing since the other one will simply take up the slack.

Gas hot water heaters should have the pilot light orifice and burner area cleaned out periodically. You should also check that the chimney venting the burner is in good condition and sufficiently insulated where it passes through a wall. Naturally there should be no gas leaks — check by smell not by waving a lighted match around, most gas has an added odor to aid in leak detection.

One last thing to check is the pressure relief valve. Many heaters have one of these, usually located on top. Their purpose is to leak should anything malfunction inside the tank, and by leaking prevent an explosion. If it appears to be continuously leaking, call a repairman, for it may need an adjustment to withstand a higher pressure — or there may be something wrong inside!

AUGUST

LEAKS AND BLOCKAGES

To complete the check of the plumbing system, all that remains now is to methodically inspect all faucets to ensure that all may be closed with no drips continuing, and all drains, traps, and waste lines to see that there are no leaks here either, and that everything does in fact drain away efficiently.

This checkup must include not only sinks and tubs, but also things like dishwashers, washing machines, sprinkler systems, toilet fixtures, and outside faucets.

One other often forgotten part of the plumbing system is the vent stack. This is a pipe which rises from the main drain of the house and usually exits high on the roof. Its purpose is to provide an escape for air and sewer gas which might otherwise find its way into the house, and prevent air locks from blocking the draining of various fixtures. It is worth a trip to the top of the pipe once in a while to make sure that it has not become clogged or blocked by birds' nests or other debris.

VENT STACK

THINGS TO CHECK	YEAR								
STORM DOORS & **WINDOWS** *for* condition & readiness									
REGULAR WINDOWS *for* glass & putty, paint & rot									
WEATHERSTRIPPING on doors & windows									
CRACKS & JOINTS for caulking									
HEATING SYSTEM for cleanness & operation									
CHIMNEY *for* cracks, dirt, spark arrestor, & flashing									

ANNUAL CHECKLIST OF HOME REPAIR FOR **SEPTEMBER**

S E P T E M B E R

STORM DOORS & WINDOWS.
WEATHERSTRIPPING.
CAULKING.
ON HEATING SYSTEMS:
ELECTRIC BASEBOARD,
FURNACE SYSTEMS,
CHIMNEYS.

SEPTEMBER

S eptember sees Labor Day in America and Michaelmas in Britain, both marking the end of the summer season, although summer weather can often stretch on a good deal longer. Nevertheless, it is time now to begin indirectly preparing the home for Winter, while good weather still permits certain outdoor jobs to be done.

STORM DOORS AND WINDOWS

You may not want to exchange the screens for storm doors and windows quite this early — the nights can still be warm enough for windows to be left open and there are still plenty of moths and other night insects flying around eager to investigate your burning lights — but now is the time to make sure they are ready, and while you are at it, it is also a good idea to check the regular windows.

SEPTEMBER

Although it is proving more efficient to build houses with windows comprised of permanent double glazing, to which screens can be added as needed, most houses still rely on separate storm windows (and doors), fitted during the cold season, to improve the insulation. Taking these windows in and out every year exacts a toll, and since their efficiency is largely governed by how well they fit, it is important to check that they are in good repair.

Most importantly, of course, they must have glass — and the glass should have no cracks, and be well fitted in its sash. It is annoying to have to replace a large pane of glass because of a small crack in one corner, but heat is lost this way. It may be possible to run a small bead of clear epoxy glue over the crack but replacement is best — besides, all is not lost since the damaged pane can always be recut to fit a smaller frame somewhere else.

CRACK IN GLASS

The glass is set in the frame, properly called the sash, either with putty, fast disappearing because of its poisonous lead content, or synthetic glazing compounds, which have the advantage of not becoming hard and falling out as quickly.

H owever, even glazing compound is not permanent and will eventually deteriorate. When sections crack and fall out, the window should be reglazed. The operation is easy and will prolong the life of the sash, make it more effective, and give you a wonderful feeling of righteousness and smugness when later on Winter storms are beating on the glass. The procedure is as follows. First, remove all the remaining putty or glazing compound. If the glass is broken and is to be replaced, break it even more and carefully remove the remaining shards. This will facilitate the removal of the putty. If you are merely reputtying and intend to reuse the glass you must be more careful. In either case, remove the little metal pins or clips (called glazing points) which hold the glass in its sash.

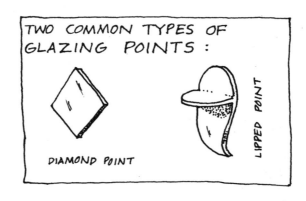

TWO COMMON TYPES OF GLAZING POINTS:

DIAMOND POINT

LIPPED POINT

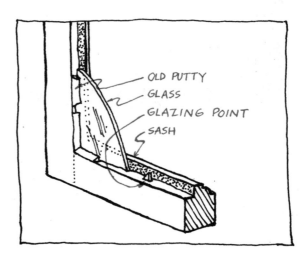

OLD PUTTY
GLASS
GLAZING POINT
SASH

With an old chisel, scrape clean the recess in the sash where the glass fits. This recess is called the rabbet. Ideally the rabbet should now be painted, or given a coat of linseed oil if putty is going to be used instead of glazing compound, but in any event a thin bead of putty or compound should be laid in the rabbet. This step is most often skipped with the result that the window simply has to be reglazed that much sooner.

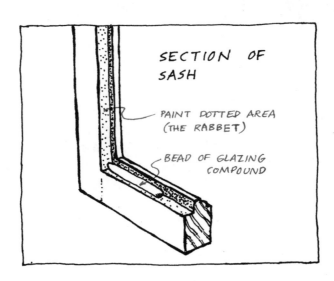

SECTION OF SASH

PAINT DOTTED AREA (THE RABBET)

BEAD OF GLAZING COMPOUND

Now install the glass, seating it firmly against the bead of compound in the rabbet so that there are no gaps and no rattles, and secure it in place with glazing points pushed in every 10 inches or so. The lipped sort are most easily inserted, but care must be taken to ensure that while they go in close to the glass and hold it tightly, the glass is not inadvertently cracked.

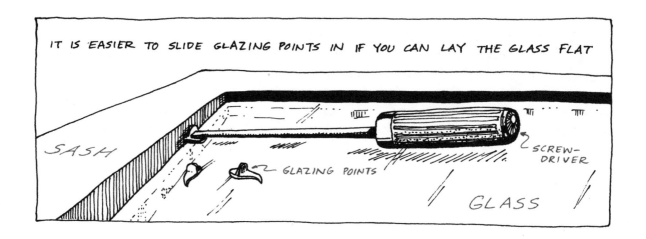

IT IS EASIER TO SLIDE GLAZING POINTS IN IF YOU CAN LAY THE GLASS FLAT

SASH

GLAZING POINTS

SCREW-DRIVER

GLASS

The glazing compound should now be made soft and pliable by rolling it back and forth between your hands, and a thin roll of it pressed against the glass, and then smoothed out by pressing firmly with a putty knife drawn along the rabbet.

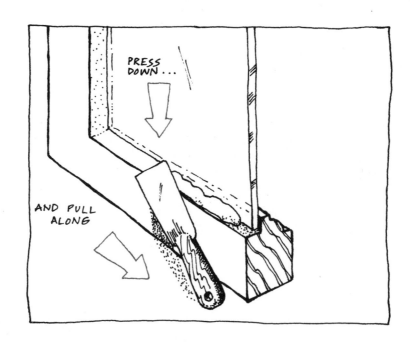

PRESS DOWN ...

AND PULL ALONG

T he last step requires a little patience - you should wait a week for the putty (or compound) to dry, and then paint it. If you don't wait, the paint may pull the putty out; and if you don't paint, the putty will eventually dry completely and fall out on its own accord.

W hen checking the condition of the storm windows, it is also convenient to similarly check all the other windows in the house. Not only should all the glass and its glazing be in good condition, but the sash and window frames should be checked for peeling paint, rot, or other damage.

WEATHERSTRIPPING

The next step is to ensure that the storm windows and doors, together with the regular windows and doors, are all draft free. This is achieved by using weatherstripping. Weatherstripping comes in many different forms from common felt to springy metal strips and plastic tubing. Choice is largely optional, but the end result should be a door or window that fits snugly in its opening.

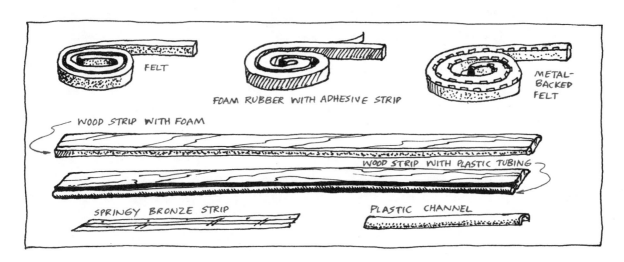

FELT
FOAM RUBBER WITH ADHESIVE STRIP
METAL-BACKED FELT
WOOD STRIP WITH FOAM
WOOD STRIP WITH PLASTIC TUBING
SPRINGY BRONZE STRIP
PLASTIC CHANNEL

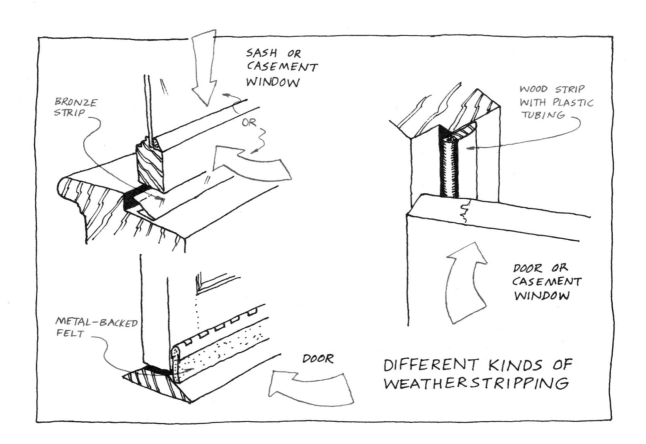

SASH OR CASEMENT WINDOW

BRONZE STRIP

OR

WOOD STRIP WITH PLASTIC TUBING

METAL-BACKED FELT

DOOR OR CASEMENT WINDOW

DOOR

DIFFERENT KINDS OF WEATHERSTRIPPING

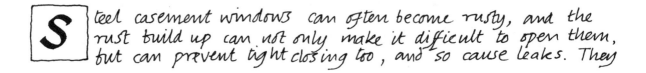

Tight fitting can go too far, however, and result in doors and windows which are hard or impossible to open. Check everything that is supposed to open and close to see that it does, in fact, open and close. Some reasons for sticking are that the hinges may be loose (see **FEBRUARY**); the door or window, or its frame, may be swollen, warped, or out of alignment and may require some carpenterial surgery; or successive paintings may have built up to too great a thickness.

Steel casement windows can often become rusty, and the rust build up can not only make it difficult to open them, but can prevent tight closing too, and so cause leaks. They should be periodically cleaned and repainted — but as with wooden doors and windows, you cannot simply paint and repaint — the time will come when some of the old paint will have to be removed.

S liding windows which slide with difficulty should have all the dirt and grime cleaned out of the grooves and then be lubricated. This can be done with silicone spray or simply by rubbing soap, or a wax or paraffin candle, on the parts which touch.

CAULKING

Defective caulking was mentioned in JULY as a contributory cause of exterior paint deterioration, but it is important in other ways too. The many openings, seams, and joints in a house's exterior are all possible sources of heat leaks. For a house to be truly efficient in terms of heat conservation all these places must be tightly sealed. Aside from first-class carpentry, and properly overlapping construction, the most effective way to close gaps is to fill them with some kind of modern caulking material.

I t is important to note, however, that large gaps may need to be filled first with a fibrous packing material such as oakum, which may be obtained from plumbing and hardware stores.

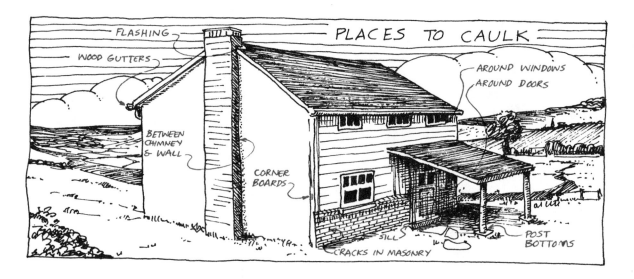

PLACES TO CAULK

FLASHING

WOOD GUTTERS

AROUND WINDOWS

AROUND DOORS

BETWEEN CHIMNEY & WALL

CORNER BOARDS

SILL

CRACKS IN MASONRY

POST BOTTOMS

T here are as many different kinds of caulking material as there are different places to caulk, though nearly all of them come in the familiar caulking cartridge designed to be used with a caulking gun. Some types, designed for interior uses such as sealing cracks around bathtubs, come in tubes.

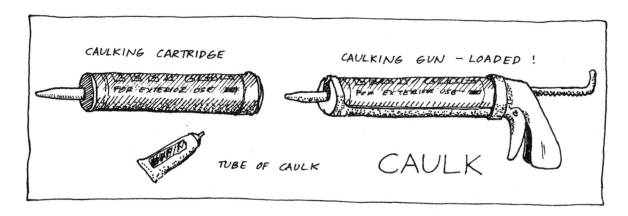

CAULKING CARTRIDGE

CAULKING GUN — LOADED !

TUBE OF CAULK

CAULK

ome of the common types of caulking materials and their specific uses and characteristics are as follows:

1. Oil-base caulking. This is the commonest and cheapest type of caulking. While it can be used for a variety of jobs, it suffers the drawback that it is not easily painted over.

2. Latex-base caulking. This can be painted over, and while it dries fast, it remains flexible and is good for many jobs.

3. Butyl rubber caulking. Although more expensive than the first two types, butyl caulk lasts much longer and is very good for use in cracks between metal and masonry.

4. Polysulfide caulking. An excellent, long-lasting material that both adheres well to paint and over which paint itself adheres well.

5. Silicone caulking. The most expensive type but also the longest lasting. However, many types of silicone caulking do not do well with paint, either over it or under it. In fact, clear silicone is often intended for paintless application, such as around bathroom tiles.

The important thing to remember about all this is to bear in mind the particular job you have in hand, and read the label carefully.

SEPTEMBER

HEATING SYSTEMS

September is definitely the month to overhaul whatever kind of heating system you have, whether it be furnace or fireplace, wood stove or electric baseboard, because you don't want to have to turn the system off to effect repairs in mid-winter.

ELECTRIC BASEBOARDS

Electric heat does not require much mainte-nance — just a periodic check to see that the thermostats are clean and operative, and that the units themselves are clean — usually a vacuum cleaning is sufficient. If anything does go wrong it is advisable to call an electrician since there is always the danger of serious electric shock to the inexperienced would-be repairer.

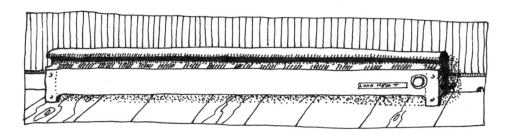

FURNACES

Coal, gas, or oil-fired furnaces are used to heat hot-air or hot-water heating systems and should be thoroughly overhauled before every heating season. Most fuel companies offer a service contract which provides you, along with delivery of the fuel, with an annual cleaning and inspection, plus a guarantee of immediate repair should any-thing break down. This is by far the best way to take care of your heating system and you should make every effort to secure such an arrangement.

However, there remain a couple of things which you should still take care of yourself. Firstly, for hot-air systems it is most important to replace the air filters whenever they become dirty. The frequency of this depends on the situation of the furnace, and how much dust and dirt there is in the air. If you are not sure, perform a monthly check while the furnace is in use. Simply remove the filter from its slot in the cold-air return and hold it up to the light — it should not be so completely blocked that you can not see any light through it, if it is replace it.

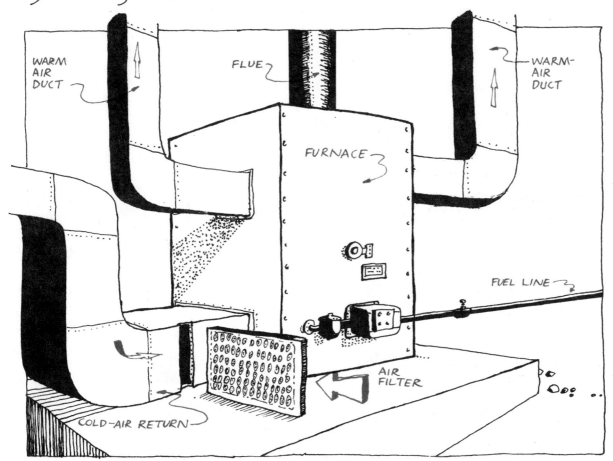

WARM AIR DUCT

FLUE

WARM-AIR DUCT

FURNACE

FUEL LINE

AIR FILTER

COLD-AIR RETURN

The simple operation of changing the air filter regularly can save a lot of money and fuel, and greatly improve the efficiency of the system.

If you have an oil-fired furnace it is also good insurance to add a cleaning and anti-condensation ingredient every time the oil tank is filled up. Usually in liquid form, it is readily obtainable at most hardware stores under various brand names.

One other thing to check is that all heat registers and grills, whether they are floor, wall, or ceiling vents, are kept clean and unobstructed.

CHIMNEYS

Potentially the most dangerous part of any combusting heating system, chimneys of woodstoves and fireplaces are especially vulnerable to disaster if ignored season after season. Aside from deteriorating masonry (see APRIL and JUNE), it is most important to keep them clean, or build ups of soot and creosote can cause chimney fires which can endanger the whole house.

The chimney can be most easily cleaned by stuffing a sack full with newspapers, adding a few rocks for weight and lowering it down the chimney from a long rope. Doing this a few times should dislodge most of the soot and creosote in the flue.

After cleaning, the masonry should be inspected for cracks or crumbling; the flashing around the roof and chimney should be inspected for holes or corrosion; the spark arrestor (if there is one) — it is a mesh cap that fits over the top of the flue — should be examined to make sure it is in good condition; and the cleanout door — usually located at the base of the chimney — should be checked to make sure that it closes tightly. One last check is to make sure the damper is working and not stuck in one position.

Metal chimneys, which ultimately rust away, must also be very thoroughly cleaned. Especially important with stovepipes is to ensure that there is adequate insulation at the point where the pipe passes through the roof or the wall.

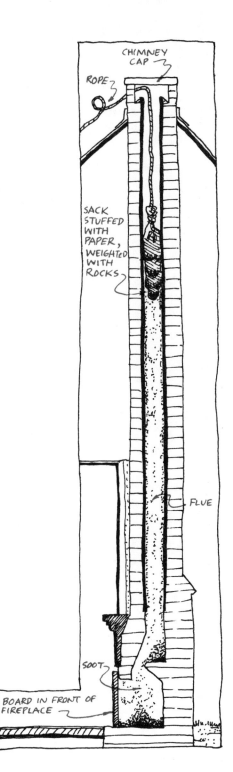

CHIMNEY CAP

ROPE

SACK STUFFED WITH PAPER, WEIGHTED WITH ROCKS

FLUE

SOOT

BOARD IN FRONT OF FIREPLACE

THINGS TO CHECK	YEAR								
FUEL TANKS for footing, lines, rust									
GARBAGE CANS for condition									
AIR VENTS for clean airflow									
INSULATION in roof, basement, & unfinished walls									

ANNUAL CHECKLIST OF HOME REPAIR FOR OCTOBER

OCTOBER

ON TANKS ·
ON VENTS ·
INSULATION ·

OCTOBER

O ctober : apples; and the first frost arrives in many parts of the country. While leaves are falling, there is often much warm weather yet, but it can be deceptive, although the animals are not so easily fooled - chipmunks begin to hibernate and many Summer visitors are off south to warmer climes. It is, in short, time to begin getting ready for Winter.

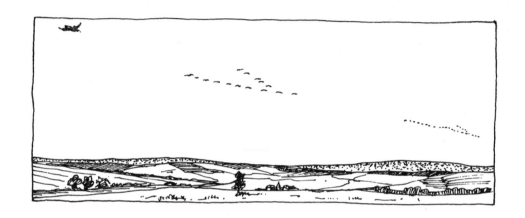

TANKS

The heating system should have been serviced and overhauled already (see **SEPTEMBER**) and now is the time to inspect the service tanks. If you have oil tanks or gas tanks (for heating or cooking), it is a good idea to check them out now before they are filled up and pressed into use in earnest.

M ake sure that all tanks sit securely on a firm base. If they are located in the basement, a firm footing is probably not a problem, but many tanks are located outside, against or near the house. If Spring mud or Winter frost causes the tanks to tilt or wobble, now is the time to rectify the situation.

OCTOBER

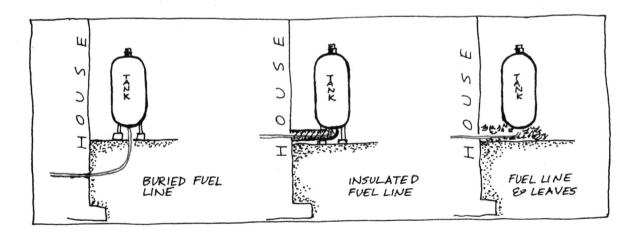

    ot only should the often fragile lines be protected from rupturing as a result of the tank moving, but they should also be insulated against freezing. This can be achieved by burying the lines, wrapping them with fiberglass insulation and an outer covering of waterproof tape, or by simply packing the area under the tank (where the fuel line comes out) with dead leaves or straw.

BURIED FUEL LINE

INSULATED FUEL LINE

FUEL LINE & LEAVES

O il tanks themselves do not last forever, eventually rusting out, often from the inside. Not only can interior rusting cause leaks, it can also cause blockages in the fuel line. Internal rusting can be held at bay by the use of an anti-condensation agent every time the tank is filled. In order to minimize condensation, oil companies often recommend that you keep your tanks full during the whole year. External rusting is more easily controlled — simply scrape it away as soon as it appears and paint the tank with a metal anti-rust paint. These paints are available in various colors, and a nice white (or red or blue etc.) tank looks better anyway against the side of the house than a grimy, oil-stained, rusty tank.

ANTI-CONDEN-SATION ADDITIVE

RUSTPROOFING PAINT

W hile you are outside checking the tanks, make sure the garbage cans are still usable and accessible. In the country many people keep the actual cans in bins to prevent dogs and raccoons from pre-sorting the garbage prior to its collection, but in the Winter a heavy snowfall can leave them inaccessible. Furthermore, lids which have cunning devices designed to foil prying fingers and noses can often freeze tight — causing much frustration in sub-zero weather.

GARBAGE CANS IN SUMMER...   — IN WINTER...!

VENTS This month check all the vents in and around the house. There can be quite a few, but unless they are clear and operable they are doing no good. Starting from the ground up, the first vents to check are the basement vents. The importance of adequate ventilation under the house has already been explained (see **APRIL**). If the basement is unheated, however, and especially if there are water pipes running through it, it is a good idea to close these vents in late Autumn and, as a further precaution, add some insulation on the inside and perhaps a board on the outside to keep the snow out. Very often, basement vents are a little way below ground level, and open into a small pit at the side of the house. In this case it helps to fill the pit with dead leaves.

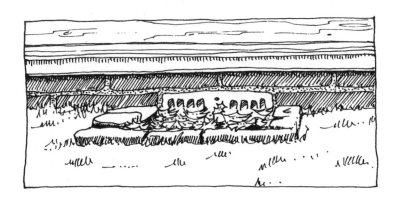

OCTOBER

The next set of vents you are likely to encounter are various exhaust-fan vents. Typically installed in areas such as bathrooms and kitchens, these need cleaning from time to time. Some have removable filters which may be either cleaned or replaced, others must be cleaned by hand. Check also that where the vent comes through the wall to the outside there is a hood or cover sufficient to keep out wind, rain, and snow. This spot is also a likely area for caulking (see SEPTEMBER).

Gas heaters and water heaters must also be vented to the outside and you should check that the various pipes, thimbles, and hoods are all in good repair, well insulated where they pass through the wall, and not rusted out anywhere.

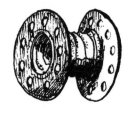

Higher up you are likely to find eave vents. These are small, screened louvers inserted in the soffit, between rafters. They permit air to flow up behind the insulation into the roof and out through the attic vents (discussed a little further on).

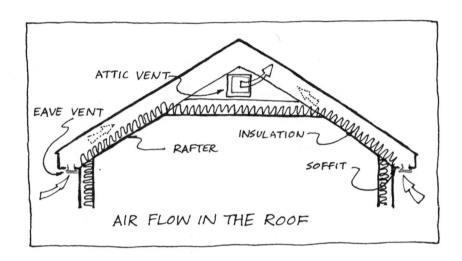

AIR FLOW IN THE ROOF

These eave vents sometimes get painted over, blocked by wasps' nests, and sometimes just fall out. If your house is equipped with these vents check that they are all present and firmly in place, and also (if you can) that the screens (designed to keep insects out of the attic) are still in good condition.

Finally, usually found in the gables, up high, are the attic vents. These were discussed earlier (see **MAY**), but a quick look now at the end of the summer can do no harm. At this time you may also check the operating condition of any heat-recirculating fans you may have in any high ceiling areas— often, a drop of oil will prevent the premature demise of such frequently overlooked appliances.

INSULATION

Although insulation is properly something that should be integral with the construction of the house and installed as the house is built, high energy costs now make it very worthwhile to pay attention to the insulation in your home to see if it can't be improved.

The first thing to realize is that insulation is worthwhile, and indeed necessary, if you consume energy for either heating <u>or</u> cooling. Its purpose is to keep heat where it belongs — either inside the house in cold weather, or outside the house in hot weather.

SUMMER

WINTER

The second thing to remember is that humidity plays a large part in comfort control (see JANUARY), and if you need insulation you also need a system of vapor barriers and ventilation.

If your house is uninsulated it will be more expensive to leave it so than to insulate it, and increasingly so as energy costs rise. Although measures such as storm windows, weatherstripping, and caulking (see **SEPTEMBER**) help, and indeed should be considered absolutely essential in any case, they do not in themselves constitute a substitute for insulation. Fortunately, there are several things you can do short of removing the interior finish of the house and installing common fiberglass rolls or batts of insulation.

Most easily, you can insulate the attic. The simplest way to do this is to pour loose-fill insulation between the joists in the attic which support the ceiling below but rarely a finished floor in the attic itself.

This loose fill is made from various materials such as ceramic fiber, glass wool, and vermiculite. The choice is yours, but it should be based on the **R**-factor rather than on the price. The **R**-factor is the number assigned to the insulating qualities of any given material. The higher the number the more efficient the insulation - regardless of its price or its size and thickness. Common values considered to be acceptable **R**-factors are **R-22** for ceilings and **R-11** for walls; but these may vary according to the severity of the climate you live in and also according to the type of heat you use — electric heat generally requires a much higher **R**-factor than moist hot-water heat for example.

Two other areas which are relatively easy to insulate are under the floor over unheated crawl spaces and basements, and the adjoining walls of unheated garages and other rooms. In these places, blankets or batts of fiberglass are easiest to install. Both come in different widths (to fit between studs or joists spaced differently) and different thicknesses (giving varying **R**-factors for different applications such as walls or floors). Batts are short lengths, whereas blankets come in long rolls. Both, however, are often backed with either foil or some specially impregnated paper in order to provide a vapor barrier. Fiberglass insulation without backing is also available for use where you want to add more insulation, and a vapor barrier already exists.

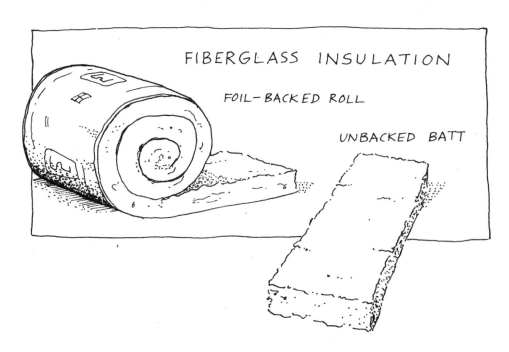

FIBERGLASS INSULATION

FOIL-BACKED ROLL

UNBACKED BATT

If you use the backed sort it should be installed with the backing facing the heated area, i.e., the inside of a house which is heated in Winter. As mentioned before, a vapor barrier is only effective if it is complete, so the value of backed insulation as a vapor barrier is questionable if you leave any spaces between adjoining strips. Therefore it is advisable to further cover the whole area with plastic sheeting (as illustrated on page **27**). It should be mentioned, though, that foil-backed insulation is probably valuable as a heat-reflecting surface.

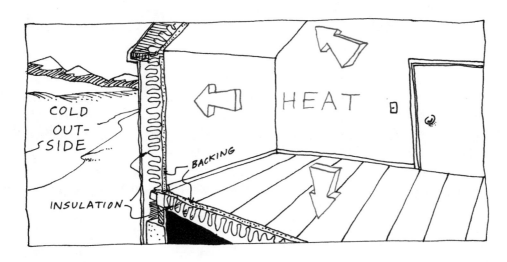

Another type of insulation can sometimes be used in places such as the underside of floors, and that type is the rigid form of insulation made in sheets of hardened foam or polystyrene. It is quite easily cut to shape, and thickness for thickness has a better **R**-factor than fiberglass—but it is also flammable, and because of this many local building codes require its use in conjunction with plaster board. This makes the job of installing it a lot heavier, more awkward, and costlier, thereby seriously reducing its advantages.

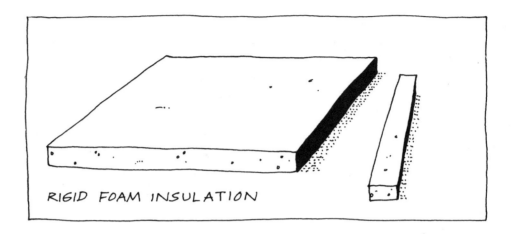

RIGID FOAM INSULATION

Probably the hardest place to insulate is in an already finished wall. In this situation you must have recourse to blown-in insulation. Small holes, which are later plugged up and painted over, are drilled into the side of the house between every pair of studs or framing members, and insulation is blown in under pressure through a hose.

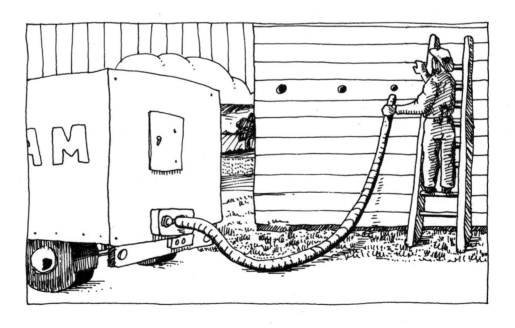

OCTOBER

There are two kinds of blown-in insulation: foam, which dries on contact and expands to fill every crevice, and loose cellulose or mineral wool, which although considerably cheaper may tend to settle over the years, leaving gaps of uninsulated spaces. Another disadvantage of this type is that little rodents love it, and they often tunnel through it and even carry some of it away to make nests with.

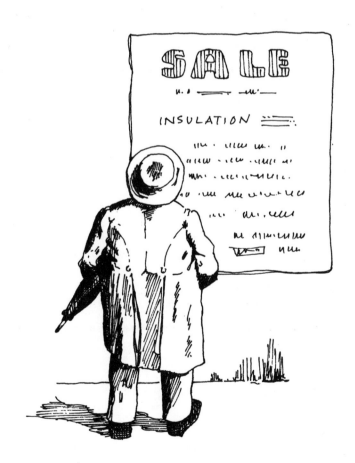

THINGS TO CHECK	YEAR									
GUTTERS & ROOFS *for leaves & branches*										
CULVERTS & DITCHES *for leaves & debris*										
DRIVEWAY *for holes & snowplow markers*										
OVERHEAD WIRES *for endangering trees.*										
FUEL TANKS & FIREWOOD *for Winter supply*										
EMERGENCY SUPPLIES *for stock*										

ANNUAL CHECKLIST OF HOME REPAIR FOR   NOVEMBER

NOVEMBER

ON GUTTERS
& CULVERTS·
THE DRIVEWAY·
OVERHEAD WIRES·
FUEL FOR THE WINTER·
EMERGENCY SUPPLIES·

NOVEMBER

N ovember sees the first of the Winter season's holidays, those holidays generally associated with being warm and snug around a cosy fire — Thanksgiving in America and Guy Fawkes' night in Britain. This is indeed the time to acknowledge Summer's final demise, despite occasional Indian Summers, and prepare in earnest for the rigors to come.

GUTTERS

Most of the leaves should be off the trees by now, and while you may not care to rake the lawn you should check a couple of other places to see that they are leaf free. The first place to look is around the roof. Leaves which fall into gutters and downspouts, and accumulate in protected areas

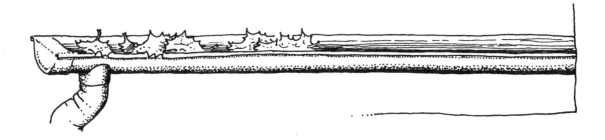

on the roof – such as at the junction between two roof slopes – can cause problems of drainage and rot and are best swept away.

LEAVES IN VALLEY OF ROOF

Go around all the gutters and make sure they are clean and all downspouts are clear. Clogged gutters can lead to ice dams (see **JANUARY**). If trees overhang the roof make sure there is no accumulation of dead leaves in the valleys or elsewhere. Needle-bearing trees such as pine and hemlock can be just as much a nuisance in this respect as broad-leaf trees. If your eaves are fitted with heat tape (to prevent ice dams), now is the time to make sure the system is operable by plugging it in. Rainbarrels and large planters should be drained and turned upside down or covered to prevent them from freezing and possibly cracking apart.

CULVERTS

The other area of potentially dangerous leaf accumulation is in the drainage ditches and culverts around the house and under the driveway. Along with a vacuum, nature seems to abhor holes in the ground, especially culverts that carry streams under driveways. As soon as the leaves are off the trees they all appear to get stuffed in the mouths of culverts, effectively blocking them and thereby setting the scene for driveway-destroying floods in the Spring and lakes of ice in the Winter. You may have to repeat the operation more than once before the snow quietens everything down but do it anyway. Go around and make sure all channels are clear.

DRIVEWAY

After having made sure that the culverts and ditches are clear, take a look at the driveway. Any potholes that may have begun to develop over the Summer should be filled in now before Winter's snow and ice have a chance to turn them into deep pits.

If you live in an area where snow plowing is a regular feature of Winter, it will be advisable to make sure that the driveway is delineated by stakes or fences so that not only will the snowplow be able to tell where it should plow but so that unwary guests in cars do not drive off into the flower beds which line the driveway so prettily in Summer but which can be completely hidden from sight after heavy snowfalls.

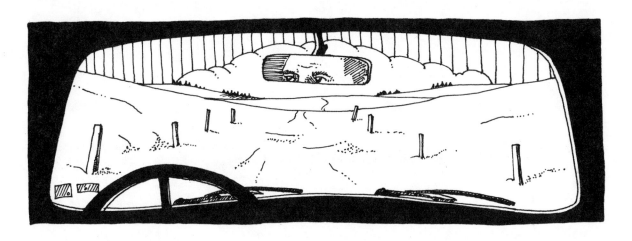

An equally important provision for the snow plow is somewhere where the mountains of plowed snow can be dumped. This can be difficult, for often the most convenient place is an adjacent lawn, but when the snow finally melts you are frequently left with a large amount of driveway gravel to rake back off the lawn. Ideally the driveway should be large enough for one area of it to accommodate the plowed snow and still leave sufficient access.

NOVEMBER

OVERHEAD WIRES

Another job which can be best done now that the trees are bare is checking that there are no overhead wires, such as telephone lines, electric power lines, or radio antennas that are threatened by overhanging branches. Power companies regularly patrol their lines along tree-lined roads, and you would be wise to check any lines on your property. A fallen tree and a broken line can spell disaster during a cold and stormy winter's night; it is much easier to arrange to have dead trees and branches removed at your convenience on a calm Autumn day.

While inspecting the various lines, cast an eye on any utility poles you may own to see that they are still sound, and, if grounded, that the ground rods are still connected and firmly in the ground.

FUEL This is the time of year to check on your fuel supply for your Winter heating needs. If you burn wood, make sure your woodpile is covered and accessible. An uncovered woodpile when snowed upon can freeze into a monolithic entity from which it can be extremely difficult to extract individual logs. Oil tanks and gas tanks should be filled and similarly protected if only to facilitate future deliveries when the snow is deep.

If you keep logs in the house, clean out the storage area often, for you may be bringing unwanted insects such as ants into the house with the firewood.

UTILITY POLE

a CUSTOMER OWNER'S LABEL
b METER BOX
c GROUND ROD

NOVEMBER

EMERGENCY SUPPLIES

. Despite all the foregoing preparations and precautions, situations can still occur when things grind to a halt through no fault of our own. Most of us today live lives which are to a greater or lesser extent dependent on a complicated life-support system further down the road. Nearly all of us are hooked into a power grid, dependent on automobiles, and reliant on a variety of municipal services which enable us to function "normally." When one of these ingredients of modern life fails, the consequences can be very uncomfortable and sometimes dangerous.

B ecause it is so easy to forget this and take things for granted, once a year run a check on emergency supplies. Most important for people who live in cold areas is a backup heating system. If you normally use electric heat or some other central heating system, but have a fireplace or woodstove, keep a supply of wood on hand. If you cannot burn wood in an emergency, keep a portable kerosene stove — with a supply of kerosene.

Loss of heat in mid-Winter supersedes all other disasters for it snowballs from discomfort to frozen pipes, eventual leaks and damage to a variety of other things.

Light is the next most important item to secure. Candles and flashlights are easy to keep, but check once in a while that your supply is adequate for a long night, and that it is located somewhere where it can be easily found in a hurry in the pitch dark. Old-fashioned kerosene lamps can be a godsend when the power lines are down somewhere, and the effect of sitting in their warm glow, with the normal hum and rumble which emanates from freezers, refrigerators, and furnaces silenced, is very peaceful and comforting.

A supply of bulbs and fuses is also a good thing to keep on hand. Dedicated survivalists may even go so far as to keep a portable generator in the basement, but most emergencies can be weathered with the few supplies listed above. One additional item which often helps is a battery-powered radio — with batteries. It is, of course, possible to continue preparing for any number of conceivable disasters by installing extra water tanks, fallout shelters, and stores of dry food, but so long as you have heat and light you will be able to weather most temporary emergencies short of earthquakes, floods, forest fires, tornadoes, hurricanes, and war or insurrection.

OUTSIDE The last thing to check before the snow arrives is the condition of the grounds and garden. Ask the following questions: have all the Spring bulbs been planted; are all tender plants such as roses adequately protected by mulching; have young evergreens been screened against drying winter winds; and have young fruit trees been surrounded with wire netting to keep out mice and rabbits?

Vegetable gardens should be cleared of refuse and planted with a Winter cover crop to protect the ground from leaching, and lawns should be no higher than two inches or the excess grass will die and form an impenetrable mat which will make Spring growth more difficult.

Finally, before you settle in for a cosy Winter, overhaul, oil, and put away the garden tools — everything from rakes and spades to power mowers, and get out the snow shovels and snow blowers.

THINGS TO CHECK	YEAR										
FUSE BOX for location & labeling											
FUSES for replacements											
OUTLETS for grounding											
PLUGS & WIRES for damage & overloading											

ANNUAL CHECKLIST OF HOME REPAIR FOR DECEMBER

D E C E M B E R

INSECTS ·
THE ELECTRICAL
SYSTEM :
GROUNDING ,
REPAIRS ·

DECEMBER

The shortest day of the year, the official beginning of Winter, the festivals of Christmas and Chanukah; all this means December. Whatever we may call it, this is the time of year when almost everything in Nature has gone away or ground to a halt. Although Christmas also marks the much older festival celebrating the return of the sun, from which point the days grow longer, the outside for most of us (excepting Winter-sports enthusiasts) is to all intents and purposes closed for the duration. It is time to stay indoors.

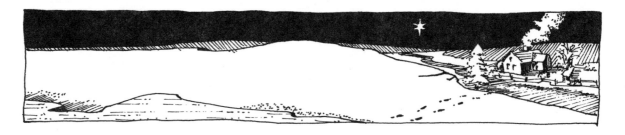

INSECTS

Most insects are either dead, with only eggs surviving the Winter to perpetuate the species in the Spring, or asleep somewhere oblivious to snow and cold. However, given the right environment — such as a nice warm attic, many can do quite well, and on a bright sunny day you can often observe groups of semi-stuporous flies walking about the window panes. Fleas, similarly protected by a domestic environment, can survive,

their numbers undiminished, in rugs and dogs. Should you discover a plague of insects at this time of year, there is a way to eliminate it without recourse to noxious insecticides. Simply open the doors and windows and let the cold in for a short while.

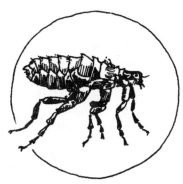

ELECTRICAL SYSTEM

Since most of us are now dependent to a greater or a lesser extent on electricity, and since most of the system is located indoors, December is a good month to check things out and make sure that you understand, if not the theory, at least where things are in your house, and how to react safely in an emergency.

The golden rule for working with electricity is never do anything until you are sure the power is off! This entails learning where the fuse box is located – for it is here that fuses or circuit breakers, and the main supply control are found.

DANGER

ypically located in some dark corner, such as a cupboard under the stairs, fuse boxes are also often found in the cellar or basement. Two things you must know are: 1. never stand on a wet or damp floor when working with the fuse box. This is especially important to remember if the fuse box is located in a basement which is liable to flood. Stand rather on some boards. 2. which fuses or circuit breakers control which circuits and appliances in the house.

deally, everything should be clearly marked and labeled in the box. You should be able to open the door and see at a glance the main breaker switch or lever — which turns off the power to the box itself — and a row of switches or fuses designated as controlling the power to different parts of the house, such as kitchen range; bedroom, furnace; hot water heater. living room; etc. The purpose of this is to enable you to fix the appropriate fuse when something goes wrong "upstairs," since all fuses (of any one type) look the same, and it is often hard to tell which one is defective, especially in the dark.

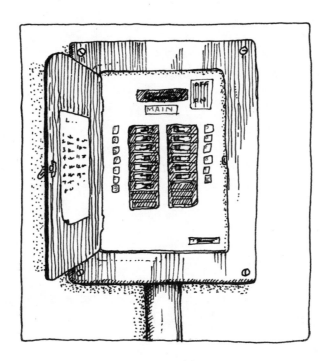

If things are not marked, it may be worthwhile to do so while everything is still working. You can either call in an electrician to trace the circuits or you can do it yourself by deductive trial-and-error experimentation. Turn everything on in the house and then note what goes out as you switch off each fuse in turn.

The actual means of disconnecting the power to each circuit in the house may be either a fuse or a circuit breaker. The function of both is to interrupt the flow of electricity, either because a potentially dangerous situation exists as the result of something going wrong, or because you want to work on part of the system.

Fuses today are most commonly one of the three types illustrated below. The plug fuse consists of a visible metal strip inside a glass screw-in unit. When the metal strip is broken or the glass become blackened the fuse is broken, and should be replaced by one of the same amperage. The dual element fuse has a spring-loaded metal strip which permits temporary overloading, such as when an electric motor starts up. Otherwise it looks like a plug fuse. The third type is the cartridge fuse. The only way to know whether this type is good or bad is to replace it with a known good fuse.

DUAL ELEMENT FUSE

OVER 60 AMPS

PLUG FUSE

UNDER 60 AMPS

CARTRIDGE FUSE

When something electrical stops working, the first job is to identify the blown fuse in the fuse box. If the lights go out in the bedroom, for example, and there is a fuse marked "bedroom," it is easy. Having first turned off items on that circuit, shut off the main power, making sure you are not standing on a wet floor and you have a flashlight handy. Then unscrew or remove the fuse in question and replace it with a new fuse of the same amperage (marked on the fuse) and then turn everything back on. It is a good idea to maintain a store of those fuses your box contains, and checking this store should be a regular job.

T he commonest reason for a blown fuse is overloading — too much going on at the same time. If it blows again after you have fixed it, but with fewer items operating, there may be damage somewhere, such as a short in a loose plug, or a frayed wire. At this point, unless you are a qualified electrician yourself, call in a professional.

T he situation with circuit breakers is much easier. These are simply switches which trip into the off position when the circuit they control is overloaded. There are two types: one kind trips all the way into the off position and needs simply be switched back into the on position (you do not need to switch off the mains); the other type trips only halfway — you must switch it completely off before you can return it to the on position.

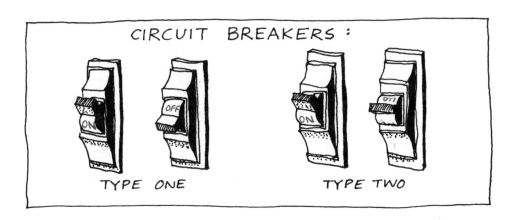

CIRCUIT BREAKERS:

TYPE ONE   TYPE TWO

I f you like the idea of circuit breakers but your house is equipped with plug fuses, you can replace them with button breakers which look just like screw-in plug fuses with a button sticking out of the center. When this kind of breaker trips, the button pops out and all you need do is to push it back in to reset the circuit.

DECEMBER

GROUNDING

You do not have to be an electrician to understand grounding, and it is definitely something you should check. Grounding means that if anything goes wrong anywhere, any loose electricity will be carried away by a ground wire back to the fuse box and from there to a ground rod set in the ground, rather than through you (with potentially damaging results) to the ground.

Modern outlets have three holes — the third one is for the ground. Modern appliances have plugs with three prongs — the third one is the ground. Such a plug in such an outlet (assuming it is wired correctly inside) provides you with protection in case the appliance should malfunction.

Older outlets which have only two holes may also be grounded inside, but require that before you can plug in three-pronged plugs you must use an adapter. This adapter will allow you to put the three-pronged plug into the two-holed outlet, but will not provide you with any grounding protection until you connect the pigtail as shown opposite.

GROUNDING ADAPTER

An appliance with a two-pronged plug may not be grounded, but if your outlets are grounded you can still achieve protection by using a Ground Fault Interrupter. You can have an electrician replace existing outlets in places where you are likely to use non-grounded appliances (such as in the kitchen or the bathroom) with GFI's (Ground Fault Interrupters), or you can use portable GFI's that simply plug into any three-prong accepting outlet.

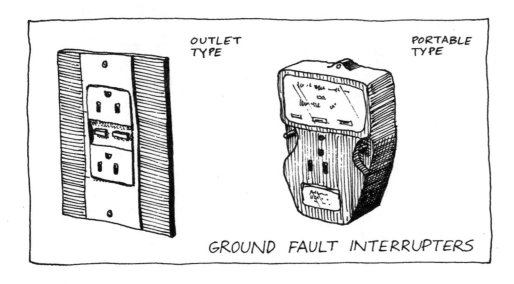

GROUND FAULT INTERRUPTERS

All of the foregoing assumes that the outlets are grounded. If they are not, you are not protected no matter how many prongs your plugs may have. This is something you should check, and it is very easy to do. All you need is a test light, available at any hardware store. Simply insert one lead of the test light into the hot-wire slot and the other lead either into the third hole or, if there are only two holes, onto the face-plate screw. The light should glow. If it does not you do not have a grounded outlet and you should have it rewired or replaced. Perform the grounding test on every outlet in the house.

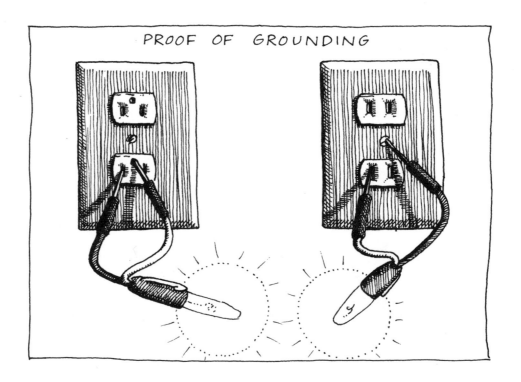

PROOF OF GROUNDING

Should you ever need to disassemble an outlet, you can use the test light to be sure that the power is off and the outlet no longer live before you start exposing its innards.

REPAIRS Most electrical repairs are best left to a qualified electrician, but there are two common repairs which can be undertaken by anybody exercising a little care. These are replacing wires and plugs on extension cords and rewiring lamps. The steps are illustrated below since a regular electrical check should be made of these items. Frayed wires, chipped or cracked plugs, bare wire showing anywhere — all should be 'decommissioned' immediately and replaced.

T here are four common types of repairable plugs for lamps and small electric appliances:

1. The lever release type. Pull up the lever in the base of the plug, insert the wire and press the lever back into place

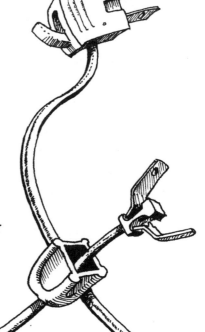

2. The case type. Separate the case from the prongs by pulling on the prongs. Insert the new wire through the base of the case. Pull the prongs apart and insert the wire into the base of the prongs. Squeeze the prongs back together again — this holds the wire tight — and replace the prongs back in the case.

3. The two-pronged screw-terminal type.

1. Remove the insulating cap.
2. Insert wire and tie the underwriters' knot.
3. Connect wires to screw terminals and replace the insulating cap.

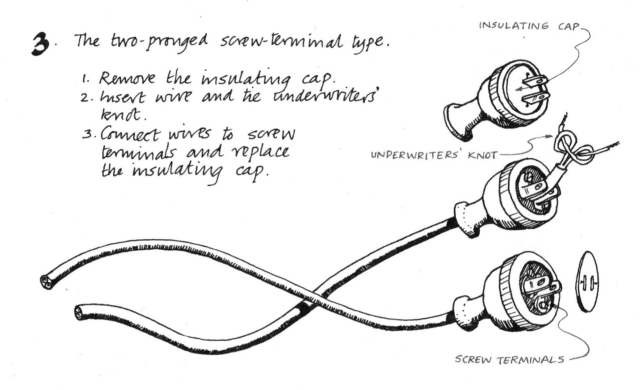

INSULATING CAP

UNDERWRITERS' KNOT

SCREW TERMINALS

4. The three-pronged grounded plug.

While it doesn't matter which wire you attach to which terminal in a two-pronged plug, there is a difference in a three-pronged plug. You must be careful to attach the green (or bare) wire to the green or largest terminal, since this is the ground. Otherwise the procedure is the same as for a two-pronged plug.

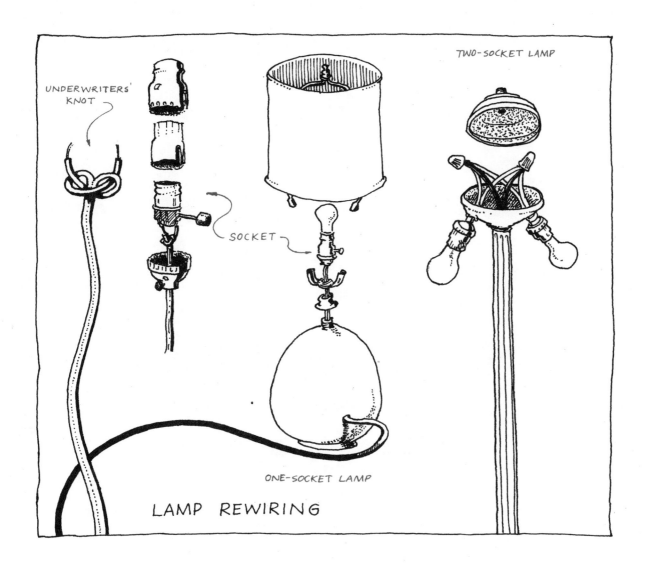

UNDERWRITERS' KNOT

SOCKET

TWO-SOCKET LAMP

ONE-SOCKET LAMP

LAMP REWIRING

One final word of caution : avoid the excessive use of extension adapter plugs to plug more than two things into any one outlet. It is ultimately possible to overload the circuit and even cause a fire. So make the inspection of outlets part of your annual check, too.

Old houses mended, cost little less than new before they're ended.

The Double Gallant, Prologue by Colley Cibber 1671-1757

BIBLIOGRAPHY

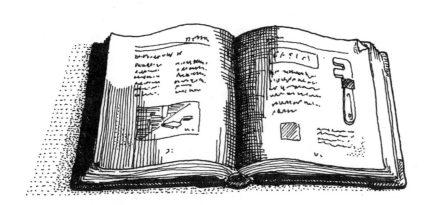

*I*f you should decide to tackle not only maintenance but actual repairs yourself, and if indeed you should desire to go on and effect alterations and additions, and then build perhaps even a whole new house, the following list of books will prove useful.

*I*f you are not too familiar with tools in general, I would refer you to my earlier book: THE ILLUSTRATED ENCYCLOPEDIA OF WOODWORKING HANDTOOLS, INSTRUMENTS & DEVICES, Simon and Schuster, 1974. Very basic carpentry skills can be gleaned from my earlier book: ILLUSTRATED BASIC CARPENTRY, Bobbs-Merrill, 1976. Intimate anatomical knowledge of a house's structure can be obtained from my earlier book: THE PARTS OF A HOUSE, Richard Marek Publishers, 1980; and how to actually build and then finish a house is explained in my two earlier books: ILLUSTRATED HOUSEBUILDING, Overlook Press, 1974, and ILLUSTRATED INTERIOR CARPENTRY, Bobbs-Merrill, 1978.

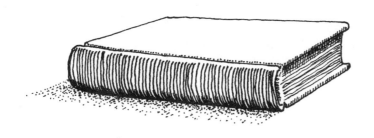

BIBLIOGRAPHY

he following books are invaluable for the different and specific areas of expertise they cover.

AUDEL MINI-GUIDE, HOME PLUMBING REPAIRS, Indianapolis: Theodore Audel & Co., 1974
    An excellent introduction to most aspects of home plumbing.

DEZETTEL, LOUIS M., MASONS AND BUILDERS LIBRARY. Indianapolis: Theodore Audel & Co., 1972
    All you need to know about residential masonry and its construction.

GLADSTONE, BERNARD, THE NEW YORK TIMES COMPLETE MANUAL OF HOME REPAIR, New York: Times Book, 1978
    Many photographs of actual techniques and much useful general information.

PALMQUIST, ROLAND E., HOUSE WIRING, Indianapolis: Theodore Audel & Co., 1975
    A complete course in the electrical workings of your house.

RAMSEY, CHARLES GEORGE, and SLEEPER, HAROLD REEVE, ARCHITECTURAL GRAPHIC STANDARDS. New York: John Wiley & Sons, 1970
    This book is the source for all technical and structural details, and is considered a standard item in all architects', builders', and designers' offices.

SCHAEFER, CARL J., and SMITH, ROBERT E., HOME MECHANICS, Milwaukee: Bruce Publishing Co., 1961
    Good basic procedures for the more technical aspects of home repair — electricity, plumbing, etc.

SUNSET BOOKS & SUNSET MAGAZINE Eds., BASIC HOME REPAIR, Menlo Park, California: Lane Books, 1975
    An instructional book for the novice who is determined to do it him- or herself.

I N D E X

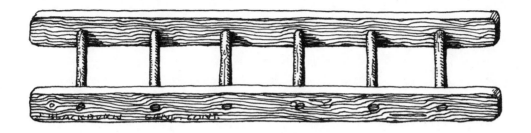

INDEX